Standing
on the
Promises

Standing on the Promises

A Woman's Guide for Surviving the Storms of Life

SUSAN WALES

with Holly Halverson

Multnomah® Publishers *Sisters, Oregon*

STANDING ON THE PROMISES
published by Multnomah Publishers, Inc.
© 2001 by Susan Huey Wales

International Standard Book Number 1-57673-796-9

Design by Chris Gilbert / Uttley DouPonce DesignWorks
Cover image by Gary Isaacs / Photonica

Unless otherwise noted, Scripture quotations are taken from:
The Holy Bible, New International Version © 1973, 1984 by International Bible Society.
Used by permission of Zondervan Publishing House

Also quoted: *The Message* © 1993 by Eugene H. Peterson
The Living Bible (TLB) © 1971. Used by permission of Tyndale House Publishers, Inc.
All rights reserved.
The Holy Bible, King James Version (KJV)
Holy Bible, New Living Translation (NLT) © 1996.
Used by permission of Tyndale House Publishers, Inc. All rights reserved.
New American Standard Bible® (NASB) © 1960, 1977, 1995 by the Lockman
Foundation. Used by permission.
The New English Bible (NEB) © 1961, 1970 by the Delegates of the Oxford
University Press. Reprinted by permission.
The Holy Bible, New King James Version (NKJV) © 1984 by Thomas Nelson, Inc.

Multnomah is a trademark a Multnomah Publishers, Inc., and is registered in the U.S.
Patent and Trademark Office. The colophon is a trademark of Multnomah Publishers, Inc.

Printed in the United States

For information:
MULTNOMAH PUBLISHERS, INC.•Post Office Box 1720•Sisters, Oregon 97759

Library of Congress Cataloging-in-Publication Data
Wales, Susan.   Standing on the promises : a woman's guide for surviving the storms
of life / by Susan Huey Wales.   p.cm.   Includes bibliographical references.
ISBN 1-57673-796-9   1. Christian women–Religious life.   I. Title.
BV4527 .W32 2001   248.8'43–dc21   00-012789

01 02 03 04 05 06 07—10 9 8 7 6 5 4 3 2 1 0

This book is lovingly dedicated
to the most wonderful parents in the world,
Mr. and Mrs. Arthur Huey Jr.

During my idyllic childhood not many storms passed my way,
but thanks to the two of you,
I was equipped with God's Word and promises
when the storms of life did find me!
Your lives are shining examples of God's excellence
in all that you do.
The lessons you have taught your children
will endure for generations.

To my mother:
Her children arise and call her blessed;
her husband also, and he praises her:
Many women do noble things,
but you surpass them all.
PROVERBS 31:28–29

To my father:
He who pursues righteousness and love
finds life, prosperity and honor.
PROVERBS 21:21

He [is] hospitable, one who loves what is good,
who is self-controlled, upright, holy and disciplined.
TITUS 1:8

CONTENTS

ACKNOWLEDGMENTS

A heart full of gratitude to my wonderful friends at Multnomah, led by the brilliant publisher with the vision, Don Jacobson.

There may be a woman behind every great man, but behind every writer is a great editorial vice president. For me, that is Bill Jensen. He has become my cherished friend. It is such a blessing to be graced with Bill's genius, enthusiasm, and wisdom.

Thanks to my good friends in editorial, Penny Whipps and Steve Curley, who worked alongside us throughout the process.

I am grateful for the artistic talents that God gave Chris Gilbert, who designed the beautiful cover.

As always, I send a big hug to the marketing and sales team, who get books into readers' hands. You are too numerous to mention but are some of my very favorite Multnomah friends!

A special thanks to Ken Ruettgers, Multnomah's editorial director, who connected me with my incredible editor, Holly Halverson. When Holly and I met it was truly an editor/author *match made in heaven!* She has brought so much wisdom and love into this project. We prayed over every word, every Scripture, and every thought in this book. Holly, meeting you was truly a divine appointment. We make a great team, even if I do say so myself!

I am grateful to my parents, Mr. and Mrs. Arthur Huey Jr., for my Christian heritage. I am also filled with gratitude and my heart holds a special place for all of the teachers, church leaders, and pastors at the First Baptist Church in Roanoke, Alabama, where I spent most of my childhood and continue to visit as an adult. The Cathedral of Saint Philip, Mount Paran Church, and The Church of the Apostles in Atlanta—where I heard such great teachings during my teenage years and as an adult—each holds a very special place in my heart.

To my dear husband, Ken, and my darling daughter, Megan: Thanks for your loving encouragement and especially for your patience while I birthed this project. You are the wind in my sails and have painted the colors in my rainbow! It has been difficult at times to survive the storms that have blown our way, but it's an honor to stand beneath God's umbrella with the two of you.

For their encouragement, I send a bouquet of love to my friends Sarah Rush and Robin Shope who read my manuscript.

Love and gratitude to all my dear friends who have survived the storms and who have shared their hearts and their incredible stories to encourage others.

Please feel free to visit me at my website: www.susanwales.com.

Safety in Storms

Man shall not live on bread alone,
but on every word that proceeds out of the mouth of God.
MATTHEW 4:4, NASB

*L*et me start with a confession. When I sensed God urging me to write a book about His promises, I hesitated. I knew the need was real. Every day I minister to friends who are hurting and asking tough questions: "Where is God in this situation? Why doesn't God help me? Will I ever recover from this? I'm a Christian, but since this happened God seems so distant—does He care? How can I acquire His strength for facing what is ahead? Can I really survive this storm?" The need for this book weighed heavier and heavier on my heart.

I finally presented the outline to Bill Jensen, the vice president of editorial at Multnomah Publishers. "Women are hurting," I told him, "even women of great faith. I've walked that path. I know the need for encouragement and hope. I understand the ravaging questions pain brings. I know the dark night of the soul—and I know that joy comes in the morning. It can be found in God's Word, in His promises. I want to share my pain as well as my victory through Jesus and His Word."

Bill shared not only my heart but also my enthusiasm for the book. He encouraged me to take on the project. "But this is a topic for a seasoned theologian," I protested. I am no authority; in truth, I am a *nobody* in the religious community: I possess no seminary degrees, no glowing credentials. I am just a woman who loves and trusts God with all her heart.

Bill assured me that I was the right person to write this book because I'm a storm survivor myself. I have struggled with most of these issues. I experienced a bad marriage, a devastating divorce, single parenthood, financial setbacks, debilitating depression, and frightening problems while raising my daughter. But I have endured. How? *Not* because I have intense faith or because I'm supernaturally strong. I survived my storms only because through each I drew closer to God. I kept turning to the foundation that my parents had established early on in my life, the Word of God. There I found the Father's promises, His forgiveness, His restoration, and the peace that passes all understanding. There I found Jesus and the healing balm of Gilead. There I found second chances. He has taught me so much through His Word, and I've grown to know His comfort so intimately that I can now thank Him for the storms— that in itself is a miracle!

So while I cannot minister to you as a theologian or explain why bad things happen to good people, I can encourage you as a friend and fellow struggler. I can assure you that if you stay in the Word and stand on God's promises, He will be faithful. He will see you through.

Storms are a part of every person's life. Pain and sorrow are as certain as the seasons. Jesus said, "Everyone who hears these words of mine and puts them into practice is like a wise man who built his house on the rock. The rain came down, the streams rose, and the winds blew and beat against that house; yet it did not fall, because it had its foundation on the rock" (Matthew 7:24–25). Does Jesus say that if we obey His words, we will not face storms?

No! He says that when the storms come, His words will make us strong against the wind and rain that rages. He promises that we can stand through faith. My desire with this book is to help you begin to build your life on the rock-solid certainty of God's promises. You will be prepared when they come, strengthened if you are facing one today.

Let me make one thing clear: Even with my knowledge of God's goodness, at times I still struggle. I cry, I search, I doubt…but I also praise, I believe, and I stand. Storms still come—often. But when times get really tough, I find relief by digging a little deeper into the Word. It gives me hope, it builds my faith, and it assures me of my Father's love. As Christians, we are incredibly blessed to have this instruction manual for guidance through life. Every problem has a solution in God's Word!

In the chapters that follow, you will read parts of my story as well as the stories of a number of women I know. I have changed some names and details to protect privacy, but these are all true stories. Each woman in this book found herself in the midst of the gale-force winds and pelting rains of a personally shattering storm. And each woman found her safest shelter in God's promises.

What comfort I find in His Word and in the Lord Himself! One of the greatest lessons I've learned in my walk through the Bible is to seek not healing, but the Healer; not love, but the Lover; not gifts, but the Giver; not answers, but the One who knows all the answers. The God of all comfort will comfort us even when there are no explanations.

In this book I also share promises and ways to apply them in each type of challenge. If you stand on the promises, your circumstances may not change—but your attitude will. You will come to understand, and find strength in, the fact that though life promises us storms, Jesus promises His *presence*. We never have to endure alone.

To release promise power in your life, practice the eight P's:

1. PLAN. Seek God's *plan* for your life, commit His plan to Him, and walk that plan in excellence. "There is no wisdom, no insight, no plan that can succeed against the LORD" (Proverbs 21:30).

2. PREPARATION. *Prepare* for storms by studying God's Word. Know the God you serve—discover His compassion! "Run in such a way as to get the prize. Everyone who competes...goes into strict training.... We do it to get a crown that will last forever" (1 Corinthians 9:24–25).

3. PROMISES. Stand on God's *promises.* "Your promises have been thoroughly tested, and your servant loves them" (Psalm 119:140).

4. PRAYER. *Pray* without ceasing for all your needs. "If you believe, you will receive whatever you ask for in prayer" (Matthew 21:22).

5. POWER. Rely on God's *power,* not your own. "You are the God who performs miracles; you display your power among the peoples" (Psalm 77:14).

6. PERSEVERENCE. *Persevere* through the tough stuff. Be "tough stuff" spiritually! "You need to persevere so that when you have done the will of God, you will receive what he has promised" (Hebrews 10:36).

7. PRAISE. *Praise* God in every situation, even if it is only for one thing a day. "Be joyful always; pray continually; give thanks in all circumstances, for this is God's will for you in Christ Jesus" (1 Thessalonians 5:16–18).

8. PEACE. Find God's *peace* by trusting Him to take care of you. "Peace I leave with you; my peace I give you.... Do not let your hearts be troubled and do not be afraid" (John 14:27).

Yes, I want to write this book. I want to encourage you who are suffering, who face the stinging winds and blustery rain of a storm. I want to stand with you when there are no obvious answers. I want to help you find the only answer that really matters. I want to be your friend in the winds that blow your way, and invite you to come under the shelter of Jesus Himself.

Come along and stand with me on His promises. I will share my umbrella with you.

Standing on the Promises

Standing on the promises of Christ my King
Through eternal ages let his praises ring
Glory in the highest, I will shout and sing
Standing on the promises of God.

Standing on the promises that cannot fail
When the howling storms of doubt and fear assail
By the living word of God I shall prevail
Standing on the promises of God.

Standing on the promises of Christ the Lord
Bound to Him eternally by love's strong cord
Overcoming daily with the Spirit's sword
Standing on the promises of God.

Standing on the promises I cannot fall
Listening every moment to the Spirit's call
Resting in my Saviour, as my all in all
Standing on the promises of God.

R. Kelso Carter

CHAPTER ONE

WAITING FOR THE KNIGHT TO COME

If winter comes, can spring be far behind?
PERCY BYSSHE SHELLEY

*I*s everyone supposed to marry?"

I hear this question time and again from single women and men who long to tie the knot, as well as from their concerned parents and grandparents. Personally, I believe that God intends for most of us to have a partner. We are all born with the desire for human contact, and as we enter adolescence, our bodies produce hormones that ignite a desire to partner with the opposite sex. Furthermore, we have God's Word on the topic: When He created the first human, He clearly stated, "It is not good for the man to be alone" (Genesis 2:18), and He created woman. God calls some to singleness to focus on other endeavors, but if you experience a deep, unchanged longing for a mate, one is probably awaiting you.

That said, let's be honest: Waiting for Mr. Right can seem like slow torture. Maybe you felt ready to marry five, even ten years ago, but no eligible male appeared on your horizon. Perhaps you suffered through an unhappy marriage and decided this time to wait for God's best, but he hasn't shown up yet. Maybe you've watched many of your friends marry in lavish ceremonies, and you're ready to throw in the bridesmaid's towel. Whatever your situation, know that I know—and God knows—that this *is* a storm. He has provided promises that you can stand on while you wait.

Friend, we serve a loving God. Jesus affirmed, "If you, then, though you are evil, know how to give good gifts to your children, how much more will your Father in heaven give good gifts to those who ask him!" (Matthew 7:11). God wants to satisfy His children's desires. He wants to provide the best mate for you; He has no intention of depriving you of any good thing (Psalm 84:11). With that in mind, take a stand on these rock-solid words from your good Father Himself.

GOD HAS A PLAN JUST FOR YOU—AND IT IS GOOD

Key Promise: "For I know the plans I have for you," declares the LORD, "plans to prosper you and not to harm you, plans to give you hope and a future" (Jeremiah 29:11).

As coauthor of *A Match Made in Heaven*, a treasury of true stories relating God's wondrous ways of bringing men and women together, I have met hundreds of single readers who wonder, *Am I ever going to meet anyone?* I have also spoken with parents and grandparents who long for their children and grandchildren to marry, and who are perplexed when the wait extends beyond their understanding. What each person really wants to know is, *Does God have a plan? I can't see one!*

At one time in my life I asked the same question. As I shared in the introduction, I experienced a devastating divorce and became a single parent. For seven years I labored alone—you readers who are raising children alone know what I mean—and I longed for help. But I knew that finding a good man was beyond my human capabilities.

I decided to stand on God's loving promises. His Word clearly states that He designs His own special plan for each of us. Just as He presented Adam to Eve, He can and will introduce your husband to you. His Word tells us that we are unique, that His eyes have been upon us from the very start of life.

Oh yes, you shaped me first inside, then out;
    you formed me in my mother's womb. . . .
You know me inside and out,
    you know every bone in my body;
You know exactly how I was made, bit by bit,
    how I was sculpted from nothing into something.
Like an open book, you watched me grow from conception
        to birth;
    all the stages of my life were spread out before you,
The days of my life all prepared
    before I'd even lived one day.

PSALM 139:13, 15–16, *THE MESSAGE*

From real-life experience, I can tell you that He has designed a plan just right for *you*. As a perfect example, I would like to share how He brought my husband, Ken, into my life.

My friends were always after me about getting out to meet single men. "How are you ever going to meet anyone if you stay home all the time?" they would ask. I was still attending a couples' Sunday school class; as a mother and a career woman, the singles' classes at the church just weren't for me. I couldn't find time in my schedule for all of their activities.

I probably don't need to tell you about my blind dates—haven't you had a few doozies yourself? First there was Indiana Jones, who almost drowned me in a river on one of his "adventure dates." Then came the disco king, who swung me around on the dance floor so forcefully that I couldn't move for two days. I finally left him flat on the floor, doing the crocodile! My favorite date of all time, however, was the one who took me to the Rat River Deer Hunting Club for a barbecue. Need I say more?

Consequently, when my friends pestered me about making myself available to eligible bachelors, I always told them the same thing: "God knows that if He wants me to marry, He's going to have to drop a man out of an airplane at my feet!" I knew that this sounded ridiculous and presumptuous, but I was only trying to make a point. I believed in God's provision, not my own finagling.

I was confident that God understood me completely. Running a business and a home, juggling finances, spending time with the Lord, and raising a child on my own overwhelmed me. There just weren't enough hours in the day for me to get out there. I couldn't have added another item to my list. It was actually a relief to let God handle the detail of bringing me a soul mate.

I believe that the way I met Ken illustrates God's sense of humor, as well as His love, His devotion, and His understanding of us as individual children. Are you sitting down for this? God literally dropped Ken out of an airplane and deposited him at my feet! You guessed it: I met my future husband when I picked him up at the airport. He was standing at the curb when I drove up. I knew the minute Ken climbed into my car that he was the one God had chosen for me. It was as though God had shone a light from heaven down on him.

Friend, you may be at one of your darkest hours today. So was I, as I struggled through divorce and single parenting. Some days I could hardly see, let alone pray, through the pain. Right now you may carry the weight of unshed tears because your future looks dim and you feel completely hopeless; but believe me, dear friend, there's glory over the hill! A plan far more wonderful than you or I could ever dream up is *in progress* in the Lord's hands. Let my story encourage you.

> *Lord save us all from…a hope tree that has lost*
> *the faculty of putting out blossoms.*
> MARK TWAIN

Another Piece of the Puzzle

I need to add a little side note. During the painful final years of my first marriage, God was already at work. When I met Ken, God revealed to me how every single piece of the puzzle fit into the big picture. Not one single moment of my life had been wasted.

Case in point: Years ago as I was standing in a long line one day at the dry cleaners', my toddler squirmed out of my arms. Before I could recapture her, she had knocked over a stack of secondhand books in the corner. A sign on the table read *Books for Sale—25¢*. Just as I reached my daughter, I watched her gleefully rip the cover from a book. Irritated, I wondered, *What book have I bought now?* As I glanced at the cover I noticed it was *Something More* by Catherine Marshall. I scolded my two-year-old, gathered my laundry, paid a quarter for the damaged book, and returned home.

Later that evening as I was waiting for my husband to come home, I pulled out the book. It was yellowed and torn, a couple of pages were missing, and I almost threw it out—but the title *Something More* called out to me. I desperately needed *something more* in life.

That book was significant in guiding me on a deeper walk with the Lord, as well as providing integral understanding of God's plan for my life. It led to my discovery of other great books by Catherine Marshall, who through her wise writing gently mentored me. I drafted numerous letters to Mrs. Marshall telling her how much her books meant to me, but I never sent one. My intentions were good, but I couldn't find the appropriate words to express my gratitude.

While listening to a radio broadcast in 1983, I learned that Catherine Marshall had died. I burst into tears. Not only did I feel as though I had lost one of my dearest friends; I also deeply regretted that I hadn't let her know just how much God had used her work to influence my life. I immediately fell to my knees. *Lord, please forgive me for never thanking Catherine Marshall for her writings.*

It's too late now, but if there is ever anything I can do for her while I am on this earth, here I am, Lord.

When I rose from my prayer, I felt slightly ridiculous. What a presumptuous offer! It must have appeared silly to the Lord. What could I ever do for Catherine Marshall?

Enter Ken. At the last minute, I had reluctantly agreed to accompany my friend Francine to pick him up at the airport. Ken was coming to town as a guest speaker for a film event, and she had volunteered to chauffeur him.

The moment Ken stepped inside the car it was as though God had opened up the heavens. Immediately He told my heart that Ken was the one for whom I had been waiting. I felt the presence of God, but I also felt cautious; I didn't dare tell Ken that God was, at that very moment, telling me that he was to be my husband—he probably would have jumped from the moving car! Instead, I followed Mary's example in Luke 2:19: I treasured up all these things and pondered them in my heart. I waited to see how God's plan would unfold.

As we became better acquainted I discovered that Ken, a film and television producer, had a dream of making Catherine Marshall's book *Christy* into a TV series. I had originally heard of this idea from my friend Francine, and we had been praying about it for over three years. Together we had asked God to bring this godly project to fruition. Who knew—except the heavenly Father, of course—that God would take me up on a sincere offer I had made at Catherine Marshall's death, more than seven years earlier? I did not reveal my prayer to Ken until much later, when he proposed. It was a far more powerful confirmation then than it would have been when we first met.

And sure enough, when Ken produced the *Christy* series for CBS Television, my background knowledge of Marshall's writings proved invaluable. God had been at work on a beautiful, amazing plan; Ken and *Christy* were confirmations of this.

A Surprise at Every Turn

Here's another piece of the puzzle: When Ken and I became engaged, another good friend and longtime prayer partner, Ann Perdue, called to congratulate me. She casually asked if I remembered our praying several years earlier for a man who was about to undergo serious surgery.

"Ann, I'm so glad you mentioned that," I said. "For years I have wanted to ask you how his surgery came out—every time you and I spoke, I meant to inquire about it! I felt that our prayer for him was so special and anointed."

Ann laughed. "Why don't you tell *me* how his surgery came out? You're marrying him!"

It turned out that the doctor had removed a benign tumor near Ken's vocal cords, a surgery that could easily have resulted in the loss of his voice. I was stunned and humbled by this discovery. Our loving Father had allowed me the opportunity to pray for my future husband in his hour of greatest need, *six years* before I had even met him!

As I'm sure you can imagine, I am neither the first nor the last to experience God's perfect provision. Read on!

> *Faith is putting all your eggs in God's basket, then*
> *counting your blessings before they hatch.*
> RAMONA C. CARROLL

CHANCE—AS ARRANGED BY GOD

The love story of our dear friends, Dr. Steve and Carole Berry, clearly illustrates the trustworthy leading of the Lord. Chance has nothing—and Fatherly love everything—to do with it.

As a young man, Dr. Berry spent one summer helping to film a documentary in Switzerland. He frequently drove between St. Moritz and Zurich. On one particular day, however, he decided to take the tram. Just as it was pulling out of the station, he noticed a young woman running alongside. The driver stopped, and she boarded the tram, choosing the seat directly in front of Steve.

Steve was immediately enchanted by this lovely young woman, who radiated grace and charm. As his stop passed by unnoticed, he racked his brain for something to say to her. Every line that came into his head seemed unworthy of the stunning creature before him. And there was another problem: Steve didn't speak any of Switzerland's three official languages. What if she couldn't understand him?

Then the stranger pulled out a book. Peering over her shoulder, Steve realized with relief that it was written in English. As the next stop approached, Steve knew he had to hurry in case the woman got up to leave. In panic, he blurted out, "Is that a book you're reading?"

She looked down at the book, puzzled, then back at Steve. "Yes," she said and returned to reading.

You might think that Steve would have let that end the matter, but he was entranced. He took another stab at conversation. "I notice that you're reading in English. Are you from England?"

"No."

"Scotland?"

"No."

Steve went on to list every English-speaking country he could think of. To each query she replied, "No." Stumped, Steve finally asked where she was from.

"Switzerland." Her eyes danced merrily.

On any other day, Steve notes, he probably would have let humiliation silence him at that point. Instead he asked, "Would you like to go out for a cup of tea?"

Her expression was a mix of curiosity and pity. "I have a previous engagement."

Steve gave up making conversation. But when the woman rose

to depart from the tram, Steve followed her. By now he was miles from his intended destination.

Gathering his final shred of courage, he again asked her, "Are you sure you won't go out for a cup of tea? For ten minutes? Could your appointment wait ten minutes?"

For some inexplicable reason, she said, "All right." During the course of their conversation, Steve discovered that this young woman, Carole, was as lovely to talk to as she was to look at. One tea date led to another and finally, months later, to a proposal. Steve and Carole married in January 1974.

In the quarter-century since, Steve has often reflected on the "foreign" impulses he followed that day, the absurd risks he took. What if he hadn't chosen to ride the tram, opting to drive as he usually did? What if Carole had missed the tram—suppose the driver hadn't stopped for her? What if Steve hadn't mustered up the courage to speak to her? What would have happened if Carole's indifference had caused Steve to give up after her first curt reply? What if Carole hadn't changed her mind about having tea with him?

This story illustrates the importance of seeking and following God's leading even when it is unexpected and maybe a little crazy. This story is *not*, however, a suggestion that you go "naming and claiming" a husband. You really have to wait on the Lord and receive confirmation. I doubt that anything upsets a guy so much as having his future dictated to him.

A word of caution here, dear friend—may I speak frankly? Ken tells me that when he was single, many Christian women whom he dated would tell him, "The Lord told me that you are to be my husband." Ken would gently say, "Well, the Lord hasn't told *me* that." Be careful to wait on God. If He doesn't speak to both parties, it isn't His plan at work.

When God puts two people together, their union is ordained. No one should have to plan, struggle, fret, or manipulate. This doesn't mean that the relationship will flow without ripples of conflict. Love usually blossoms over time; every couple has disagreements, finds irritating personality traits in each other, and must learn to balance conflicting time schedules. Sometimes couples break up and get back together a few times before God's plan is made clear. Friend, time is on your side when you're seeking God's will for a mate. Wait for His signs.

Steve's experience was quite unusual. And our own eagerness to discover God's mate for us may lead us astray. But don't worry! As Steve and Carole's story emphasizes, God is perfectly able to bring together any two people He wants to. He won't let you "blow" an opportunity. His power and plan are flawless.

This is a sane, wholesome, practical, working faith:
That it is man's business to do the will of God; second, that God himself
takes on the care of that man; and third, that therefore that man ought
never to be afraid of anything.
GEORGE MACDONALD

WHEN TWO WRONGS MADE A RIGHT

Are you ready to hear about another extraordinary experience? Ann, a student at Harvard, reluctantly let some friends set her up on a blind date. They insisted that Bill Jones was a wonderful Christian man who shared many of her interests, including tennis.

Ann agreed to meet her blind date on a Friday evening at Harvard Square, a popular meeting place on campus. Her friends told her that he would be driving a blue Honda. When the Honda pulled up beside her, Ann smiled and introduced herself to Bill. To the surprise of both, they were enamored from the moment they met. Was it love at first sight?

After a movie, the couple discussed tennis over pizza and set a date for later that week. Then they began to talk about their faith.

Bill exclaimed, "I can't wait to tell Leslie and David what great matchmakers they are!"

"Who are Leslie and David?" Ann asked, puzzled.

"You know, Leslie and David Jordan, the ones who set us up."

"I don't know a Leslie or a David," Ann said slowly. "You are Bill Jones, aren't you?"

"I'm Bill Collier," he told her.

They burst out laughing. Ann had gotten into the wrong blue Honda! Poor Bill Jones and the other girl (whose name was Amy—Bill thought he had misunderstood when Ann told him her name) had been left standing in the square, wondering where their dates were.

The couple's mistaken encounter turned out to be a divine appointment. God hadn't made a mistake: The wrong car was the right ride after all. The Colliers have now been married for five years.

The Bible tells us that a sparrow does not fall without God's notice.
I know he will helps us meet our responsibilities through his guidance.
MICHAEL CARDONE SR.

PROMISES TO STAND ON

Promise: God will reveal His plan to you—at least as much as you need to know today. "If any of you lacks wisdom, he should ask God, who gives generously to all without finding fault, and it will be given to him" (James 1:5).

For those of you who find yourselves in the depths of despair as you read these words, let me assure you that *God has a plan for your life, and He's working it out at this very moment.* No matter how dark and how hopeless things may seem, let the pieces fall into place. Hang on, the good is coming! How do I know? Because He had a plan for my life, one far more marvelous than I ever could have devised on my own.

Even if you've messed up (and I have, too)...even if you've waited for years...even if you've nearly lost faith that God even cares...even if your circumstances seem too dark for any light to penetrate them, friend, *wait on the Lord*. One of the greatest comforts in the Old Testament is Joseph's statement, "God intended it for good to accomplish what is now being done" (Genesis 50:20). No matter what is happening in your life at the moment, remember that God can use those circumstances for the good—*your* good.

• *Ask God to show you His plan, and then pray for guidance as to how you can fulfill that plan.* James wrote, "You do not have, because you do not ask God" (James 4:2). There is no greater blessing than knowing that you are walking in God's plan for your life. God may or may not reveal to you that He will provide a mate. Whatever He says, do it. Let Him work out the details, especially that of a perfectly chosen husband. He knows just when to bring a partner to help support or fulfill your purpose.

• *Pray for your future mate!* God admonishes us to pray about everything, so take your desire before him. (And mothers, fathers, grandmothers, and grandfathers, pray for the mates of your sons and daughters and grandsons and granddaughters.) To remind yourself during the waiting period to pray for the person He has for you, and to remember God's promises, cut out a pink paper heart and put it in your Bible. Cut out a few red paper hearts and give them to loved ones who pray for you, as a reminder of your longing and of your commitment to God's perfect will. Continue seeking the Lord, offering Him *your* heart.

I was in my forties when God revealed His plan for my life. Did I ask why He waited so long? No! Did I regret all the years I spent in pursuits outside His plan? No, because as I look back on my life, I can see that before I had any knowledge or understanding, God was already using even the *tiniest* of circumstances to prepare me for His purpose. He was refining me and allowing me to walk through difficulties that were all a part of carrying out His plan in my life. I can now say *with authority* that His will is perfect.

> *Prayer is an end to isolation. It is living our daily life with someone;*
> *with him who alone can deliver us from solitude.*
>
> Georges Lefevre

Promise: Trust is always part of God's plan. "Delight yourself in the Lord; And He will give you the desires of your heart" (Psalm 37:4, NASB).

The Lord understands our need for a partner. He understands our desire to marry because it was He who created us with the ache for a mate. Unless He calls us to another purpose, we can expect that marriage is indeed part of God's plan for our lives.

Nothing can describe the pain of waiting for God to fulfill our longings any better than this Scripture: "Hope deferred makes the heart sick, but a longing fulfilled is a tree of life" (Proverbs 13:12). The cure for a "sick heart" is a fresh focus: Concentrate on the Lord and all the good He's brought to your life, and decide how to go about sharing it with others who may feel as full of pain as you do. Don't focus on what He hasn't yet brought. This is what Scripture means by "delight yourself in the Lord." While you're celebrating and serving Him, your life will be full of meaning and blessing. God will use this time to prepare you for the future and for the man He has for you. He will use this time to draw you closer to Him, to refine you, and to teach you. He will make you ready and will be preparing your mate as well, and your delight in the Father will glorify and please Him. You will find yourself comforted by His closeness and guidance and will become expectant of good things.

And, friend, if you are one He has not called to marriage, as you delight in Him, you will feel that desire lift. Your enthusiasm and fulfillment in His role for you will overcome the longing for a mate. I have seen this happen!

There are actually two ways of reading the second part of this promise. Many believe that "He shall give you the desires of your heart" means that God will give you, in return for your love and service, the things for which you long. This is a popular interpretation, and it makes sense in light of God's character. But another way of interpreting it suggests that as we delight in God, He will then plant within us the desires He has for us, and our desires will become one. This is a beautiful thought! Think of it—desiring and acting in sync with the Creator of the universe! What more fulfilling place could any of us be?

No matter which meaning the verse renders for you, the promise is clear: Put God first, and good will follow. That is a promise you can stand on every day.

In the midst of your doubts, don't forget
how many of the important questions God does answer.
VERNE BECKER

Promise: Don't put your life on hold while you wait on the Lord; you can be fulfilling God's plan this very minute. "Be very careful, then, how you live—not as unwise but as wise, making the most of every opportunity, because the days are evil.... Serve wholeheartedly...because you know that the Lord will reward everyone for whatever good he does" (Ephesians 5:15–16; 6:7–8).

Many singles today delay really living until they get married. Life passes them by while they wait for Prince Charming. They miss out on so many blessings. One of my good friends loved to entertain, but she refused to buy a dining-room table because the man she was dating had one. She overlooked many opportunities to entertain her friends in her home, just waiting for her boyfriend to propose so she could marry him and make use of his beautiful din-ing-room table. Guess what? She never married the guy. Stop say-ing, "When I get married I'm going to…" Do it now!

• *Don't put your life on hold.* Live like there is no tomorrow! Life is a journey, not a destination—so live each day to the fullest! Great teachers of faith tell you to act as if what you long for has been deliv-ered. In your case, that could mean acting as if you are getting mar-ried by preparing to be a wife. Being a wife takes preparation and study just like any other profession. Marital success never happens overnight.

In Matthew 25:1–13, Jesus told the parable of the ten virgins to illustrate the importance of being ready when He comes again. Jesus explained that of ten virgins, five were foolish and five wise. The lat-ter were those who, when they packed their lamps for the journey to meet the bridegroom, brought extra oil. When the bridegroom was delayed, the wise virgins had enough oil to see them through the wait. The foolish virgins had to leave the meeting room to buy more oil, and they missed the bridegroom completely. Guess which ones the groom took to the banquet?

• *Is there oil in your lamp?* Will you be ready when your earthly bridegroom comes? How many times have you missed a blessing or an opportunity because you weren't prepared? Get ready for marriage while you wait for God to bring your husband into your life. How?

• *Seek wisdom from an older, godly woman.* "[The older women] can train the younger women to love their husbands and children, to be self-controlled and pure, to be busy at home, to be kind, and to be subject to their husbands, so that no one will malign the word of God" (Titus 2:4–5).

An older woman whom you respect, because of her faith, can impart wonderful advice to you because she has gained wisdom through experience. Trust a woman who walks in the ways of the Lord and studies the Word.

• *Get your house in order.* "By wisdom a house is built, and through understanding it is established; through knowledge its rooms are filled with rare and beautiful treasures" (Proverbs 24:3–4). If it is your desire to marry, you should get your house ready for a groom! To get your "house in order" means evaluating and making any necessary changes in your life: in your spiritual house, in the home in which you live, in your body, in your mind, and in your spirit.

For your spiritual house: Learn the Scriptures, join a Bible study, attend Christian conferences, and go to church regularly. If you pursue a deep, radiant relationship with the Lord, by the time you marry you will have stored up wonderful treasures in your spiritual bank account. Stand in faith. For example, an older woman in a Bible study I attended told me that she placed an empty picture frame, her faith frame, on her dresser as a reminder to thank God every morning for the Godly mate that He was going to bring her. She then prayed blessings on her future husband, whose picture later filled the frame!

For your home: It should be overflowing with peace and order. Begin organizing your closets and your drawers. Clean up and decorate. Make your home inviting. You might be surprised at the effect this has.

For your financial house: Strive to get out of debt. Clip coupons to save money. Study consumer reports on the quality of products before you purchase. Learn to be a good steward of your checkbook. Devise a system for filing your receipts and other important documents.

For your physical house (body): Paul wrote strong words to us about this. "Do you not know that your body is a temple of the Holy Spirit, who is in you, whom you have received from God? You are not your own; you were bought at a price. Therefore honor God with your body" (1 Corinthians 6:19–20). This is why every self-destructive habit and abusive action is sin. Be the best that you can be: Eat wisely; exercise regularly; sleep adequately. Good physical condition makes for calmness, clearheadedness, and joy.

For your intellectual house: God's Word has another wise recommendation: "He who gets wisdom loves his own soul; he who cherishes understanding prospers" (Proverbs 19:8). Be interesting and knowledgeable! Become informed on politics, history, and social issues.

For your emotional house: Learn the art of gracious giving: "A generous man will himself be blessed, for he shares his food with the poor" (Proverbs 22:9). Look for opportunities to share your food, money, possessions, and time. Focus on the needs and pain of others, and eventually you will stop worrying about your longings.

• *Let God be God.* After all, He made us and planned good things for us to accomplish (Ephesians 2:10). Shouldn't we be willing, then, to let Him decide if and when a mate should arrive? There is so much peace in relinquishment. Lay your desire to marry on the altar and leave it there. Paul wrote:

> Don't fret or worry. Instead of worrying, pray. Let petitions and praises shape your worries into prayers, letting God know your concerns. Before you know it, a sense of God's wholeness, everything coming together for good, will come and settle you down. It's wonderful what happens when Christ displaces worry at the center of your life. (Philippians 4:6–7, *The Message*)

Let His lordship cover you, protect you, provide for you at just the right time.

Prayer is a kind of calling home every day.
And there can come to you

a serenity, a feeling of at-homeness in God's universe,
a peace that the world can neither give nor disturb,
a fresh courage, a new insight, a holy boldness
that you'll never, never get any other way.
EARL G. HUNT JR.

CONCLUSION: USE YOUR UMBRELLA

When caught in a storm, what do you wish for most? *Shelter.* My single friends, God doesn't want fear, disappointment, or dissatisfaction to rain down on and overcome you. Use your umbrella! Stand on His promises.

Let me give you more encouragement on this topic. After reading *A Match Made in Heaven,* a friend asked to meet with me and brought up the familiar question, "Do you believe that God will bring a mate into the life of every person who wants to be married?" She had read the statistic claiming that a woman over forty is more likely to be kidnapped by terrorists than to marry. How untrue this is if God has a different idea! I shared a story with her:

A doctor was concerned about a woman who was like a daughter to him. One day he was complaining to his nurse that he couldn't understand why this lovely woman was turning forty and still had not married. "I just don't believe she's trying," he said, perplexed.

His nurse looked at him and said, "It's not that easy to get married. What do you think God is going to do—drop a husband out of the sky?"

Just as the word *sky* rolled off her lips, three hang-glider pilots landed in the field in front of their office. You guessed it—the doctor's friend married one of the hang-glider pilots. There is nothing God cannot do.

As I shared this tale with my friend, a surge of faith rose within her—I could see it in her eyes. I am pleased to report that I attended her beautiful wedding just a few weeks ago.

Friend, hang on to your umbrella. Take shelter under God's care. This storm is in good hands.

Faith is the sturdiest, the most manly of the virtues.
It lies behind our pluckiest…strivings. It is the virtue of the storm,
just as happiness is the virtue of the sunshine.

Ruth Benedict

Chapter Two

When Prince Charming Falls off His Horse

A happy marriage is the union of two forgivers.
Ruth Bell Graham

The statistics, though familiar, are still shocking. At least *half* of all marriages—even Christian ones—break into irreconcilable pieces. How can this happen? The smiling couple that yesterday traversed the aisle as man and wife is today glaring at each other across the counselor's or lawyer's conference table. Joy, unity, and terms of endearment are replaced by anger, isolation, and irreconcilable differences. How could something so beautiful turn into something so ugly?

Marital discord is among the hardest of storms. At a recent Christian women's conference, most women confessed that their biggest storms could be found in their marriages. Since the source may be one spouse or both, correcting the problem can be slow going. What if one aches to change the marriage, while the other refuses to recognize the problem? What if one finds a seductress in alcohol or another substance and replaces his spouse with this new partner? What if a spouse spots greener grass in a neighbor's yard? A painful marriage is a whirlwind that inevitably catches up both husband and wife and takes them for a frightening, sometimes fatal, ride. It's a storm that lifts us off our feet and out of control....

Out of *our* control, that is, but not out of *God's* control. While our perspectives are limited to today's scenarios, His reaches toward eternity. While our power is fleshly, weak, and short-circuited, His is supernatural, boisterous, and endlessly fueled. While we look at our damaged relationships and see failures, He looks at them and sees possibilities for new beginnings.

How can we replace our marred perspectives with His hopeful one? By standing on His promises. When we invite our heavenly Father into our marriages, we find Him providing the love and transformation we could never generate on our own. Solomon wrote that "a cord of three strands is not quickly torn apart" (Ecclesiastes 4:12, NASB)—this is true if the third cord is God himself!

GOD IS THE SUPPLIER OF RELATIONSHIP GLUE

Key Promise: "The eyes of the LORD move to and fro throughout the earth that He may strongly support those whose heart is completely His" (2 Chronicles 16:9, NASB).

How do we cope with the reality that men and women are deeply different—that two imperfect human beings trying to cohabit will always produce friction? How do we deal with the disappointment that marital bliss has wound down to wedding-bell blues? Are most of us indeed doomed for failure in our marriage relationships?

I have stood in the eye of this storm. I know the weight of dark clouds that follow an unhappy union. I've seen the conflict that threatens not only peace of mind, but peace in the home. I watched the pain overwhelm my child as she struggled to understand why my husband and I couldn't live together anymore, and I experienced the death of a relationship when our goals and dreams began to clash hopelessly.

Marriage never starts out that way. It is meant to be a fruitful, flowing partnership in which two people honor each other, God, and the vows they voiced so eagerly at the altar. But let's be honest: No matter how much they have in common, two strangers will have to work to maintain a common ground. Different backgrounds, different ideals, and different experiences prove that no couple will find constant companionship a natural, easy-to-maintain state.

My own history supports this. As I've described, I suffered through a painful marriage and then struggled as a single mom for almost eight years. When Ken came into my life, I was shocked, overjoyed, and grateful for God's intervention in my lonely life. In those early days I believed that I, Mrs. Ken Wales, was blessed and highly favored and that I was going to live happily ever after with my wonderful Christian husband. All of my problems were over, and all of my dreams could begin unfolding. For the first year of our marriage I floated on a cloud.

And then guess what? I discovered that Prince Charming was both truly charming *and* merely mortal. Yes, I learned that to keep even a God-ordained relationship working smoothly, I would have to do some giving in, giving up, and giving over—to God. All of us have periodic bouts of doubt and disillusion concerning our marriages. At one time or another, the love bubble bursts for everyone. But I can confirm that God's promise is true: He does strongly support those whose hearts are completely His. He empowers the wife who seeks His will and His help. Friend, your troubled relationship is construction material for God. With the right tools—especially your commitment to His guidance—He can build a lasting, lifelong relationship. He is the glue that you need.

We would do well to return to Eden, where man, woman, and relational woes had their beginning. There we can learn some wonderful things about our Creator. Remember how God formed all the creatures of earth, and earth itself, and considered them all good? As I mentioned in the previous chapter, one thing seemed out of place:

"It is *not* good for the man to be alone. I will make a helper suitable for him" (Genesis 2:18, emphasis mine). God sensed Adam's loneliness, and He understood his need. So while Adam slept, God fashioned a woman from one of his ribs. Imagine Adam waking from his sleep and discovering a beautiful creature beside him. What a lovely surprise! Woman is the completion of God's divine design.

Our Father in heaven ordained marriage from the very beginning. God completed man by giving him woman and placed Himself at the center of their relationship. That's good news, ladies! Men really do need us. God created us to fulfill that need—He provided where Adam could not provide for himself. God cared about Adam's solitude.

A second truth comes from Genesis. Sometime after their union, Adam and Eve discovered sin. They accepted it willingly, even greedily. And then they faced the consequences—banishment from the Garden, knowledge of their nakedness, and the pressure to cope with imperfection. But again we see God providing what humans couldn't: He gave them a new home. He clothed them. He ultimately provided perfection in His Son, Jesus, to cover for our failings. Friend, the key to any need in our lives, be it something financial or something relational, is God. He is the only one who can outperform the best among us. Where there is hate, He can sow love. Where there is fighting, He can sow harmony. Where there is separation, He can sow togetherness. In times of marital discord, let us turn to Him for the glue—and the guidance—that we need.

> *We are the wire; God is the current.*
> *Our only power is to let the current pass through us.*
> CARLO CARRETTO

WHEN CHRISTMAS CAME TO STAY

My friend Robin's mother, Pearl, chose to remain in a difficult marriage, but she never stopped praying for her husband's salvation.

Because of her unwavering faith, she experienced amazing, God-ordained results. I'll let her tell the story.

Peering out through the living-room blinds into the dark street, waiting for my husband to come home from work, I hoped that he would choose my warm dinner at our kitchen table over a bottle's cool neck at the neighborhood bar. I'd spent many sleepless nights standing at the window, searching the street for a figure coming toward the house in the moonlight. It was a familiar scenario in our home.

In discouragement I would pace the floor, praying for an answer. My friends and family asked why I stayed with my husband. When the children were young, the answer came easily: "Robin, my daughter, looks at me with huge eyes and begs me not to take her daddy away from her." Even as they grew older, though, my answer remained simple: My wedding vows were real to me. I had promised to stay with this man for better *and* for worse.

"Worse" took on more faces as the years passed. My husband had multiple affairs, a side effect of putting in so many hours at the bar. In spite of this, I chose to remain in the marriage and stood on God's promise to abide in hopeless situations. Daily I clung to the Scripture, "We do not lose heart. Though outwardly we are wasting away, yet inwardly we are being renewed day by day. For our light and momentary troubles are achieving for us an eternal glory that far outweighs them all" (2 Corinthians 4:16–17).

A particular story stood out to me, the one in Acts where Paul and Silas told their jailer, "Believe in the Lord Jesus, and you will be saved—you and your household" (Acts 16:31). While I knew the jailer's belief could not take the place of his family members' individual decisions for Christ, I understood his call to lead the way. I believed that this instruction was directed toward me as well, that perhaps by my example of faithfulness my husband would find his way to faith.

There were times when I thought my family was awash in my husband's drinking problem, but I held onto the Savior with all my might and did indeed sense Jesus' renewal. I felt Paul's instruction keenly: "If a woman has a husband who is not a believer and he is willing to live with her, she must not divorce him. For the unbelieving husband has been sanctified through his wife" (1 Corinthians 7:13–14). I knew that I might be my husband's only hope for salvation. If I walked out, he might never find Jesus. I felt that it was my calling.

One Christmas Eve the children and I began baking cookies and decorating the tree. I longed for my husband to join us peacefully for the celebration. I could hear him in the bedroom snoring as we placed our gifts beneath the glowing Christmas tree. Music lauding Jesus' birth flowed from a record on the stereo. My spirits were lifted; at least he was home.

Please give us a quiet Christmas, I prayed. How long had it been since we had experienced peace in our home? Bottles of liquor had choked our family until there was little joy left, little reason to celebrate. When he was sober, my husband was like a Santa Claus figure: generous, happy, loving. But when he was drunk, words of poison spilled from his lips. Now that the children were older, my daughter no longer wanted him present during our family times. He made life much too difficult for a sensitive fifteen-year-old girl.

"Let's hurry and open our presents while Dad is still sleeping," Robin suggested, obviously trying to avoid the conflict that her father so often brought to family gatherings.

A look of horror swept over her brother's face. "You'd open presents without Dad?" Russell asked incredulously.

She replied adamantly, "I sure would!"

"Not me." Russell was resolute. "It isn't Christmas without Dad being part of it."

"Why do you want to be around him?" Robin asked. "He ruins things with his drinking."

Russell turned and stomped into his room. It broke my heart that my children were suffering once again. I didn't want to see them sad. It was Christmas, the time of Jesus' birth. Anger welled up inside of me as I went into the bedroom where my husband was now snoring loudly. After several moments, I felt my daughter's hand on my shoulder.

"Russell needs his dad for Christmas, and he is getting him!" Robin said.

I didn't try to stop her. She knelt beside the bed and shook my husband, saying, "Wake up, Dad." His eyelids fluttered. "Dad, we need you to come and open gifts with us," Robin whispered.

"No. Too tired." He rolled over.

"I am coming back in fifteen minutes. The only present I want for Christmas is *you*," she told him.

We returned to the living room. Russell stood at the window, peering through the blinds. He reminded me of myself. Was he praying the same prayer? Robin crossed to him, and together they peered out the window. "Look, a star," she said hopefully.

I thought of the star of Bethlehem, announcing the Christ's birth and His offer of salvation for all. *Russell's star. Robin's star. My star. Jesus' star,* I thought. I suddenly realized that it was my husband's star, too.

After a few minutes, Robin and I went to see how her dad was coming along. He lay motionless in the same spot. "Dad, please get up!" she begged. She pulled aside the curtain in our room and pointed to the star. "Look!"

Then I saw that my husband was not asleep. Tears were streaming down his face. Something was happening.

I'll never forget Russell's expression that Christmas Eve when his dad walked into the living room. He looked as though his birthday and all of the other holidays had been rolled into one.

"I hear that you all want to open some gifts," my husband said, trying to smile.

"We sure do!" Russell was beaming, and Robin looked pleased. I felt hope welling within me.

"I love you, Dad," Robin told him, planting a kiss on his cheek. His blue eyes twinkled at her.

The gift of God in Jesus is salvation to the sinner, joy to the sad, hope to the hopeless, and peace to the tormented—everything we needed in our home. My daughter had wanted to exclude her dad from Christmas in order to have a better one, but this year Christmas was designed for him. The Lord had sent her to Dad to bring him to our celebration.

A few months later my husband lay on his deathbed, riddled with cancer. After using up most of his life, he finally handed over what little was left to Jesus. After decades of resisting God, and twenty-five years of my praying it would happen, my husband went home.

What an inspiring story of God's grace for a family nearly torn to pieces. He kept them together until the cause of the rift, Robin's dad, was willing to surrender.

I need to include an important warning here: Dear reader, while this is one of the ways in which God works, it is not the only way. God's call to each of us is unique. Some women He will call, as He did Pearl, to stay with an unbelieving husband until he finds faith in God. Other women He will call out of the marriage. If you are in an abusive marriage, treat your family's safety as paramount; then seek counseling about how God would have you follow Him in this rough period.

Read on about a woman who endured a situation much like Pearl's, but entered into it in a different way.

There are trees that seem to die at the end of autumn.
There are also the evergreens.
GILBERT MAXWELL

When the Only Way up Is Out

My friend Rita found that the only way she could help her husband was to hurt him—in the best way possible.

Falling in love with Danny, the big man on campus, was a dream come true. Even though he was a Christian, Danny was the life of every party. So when he drank heartily at his fraternity house every weekend, like all the other guys, I accepted his behavior as a natural part of college life—in other words, as something he would outgrow. I enjoyed the fraternity parties myself, though I refused to drink. As far as I was concerned, the desire to consume large amounts of alcohol in a party atmosphere was a "guy thing."

After graduation Danny got a great job, I started teaching, and we were married. I longed for the white picket fence, for babies, for backyard barbecues…but Danny was still partying with his friends. Weeknights after work he took to stopping by the local watering hole and often came home late to a cold supper and my tearful countenance. At first, Danny could soothe my ruffled feathers with his humor and charming personality, and by bedtime I would be all smiles. But it began to happen with greater regularity.

On Sundays, Danny began to sleep in instead of attending church with me. I begged and pleaded; Danny assured me that he was exhausted and that he would accompany me the following week. But the next week always found Danny begging off. I foolishly continued to hope that he would outgrow this juvenile behavior, too. When I unexpectedly became pregnant, I prayed he would become more responsible.

Danny was thrilled about the pregnancy, and we decided that I would resign from my teaching job when the baby arrived. Then Danny was fired as a result of his drinking on the job, and I had to resume my teaching career so we wouldn't lose our new home.

Things got worse. Pressure from a growing family and his lack of a job caused Danny to add drugs to his alcoholic binges. I returned home from work each evening to the smell of alcohol and Danny passed out on the living-room sofa.

I was frightened for our little family. I prayed that God would give me the guidance I needed. I didn't know how to handle this nightmare. In my desperation I clung to a promise I found during a sleepless night:

> *There is wonderful joy ahead,*
> *even though it is necessary for you to endure many trials for a while.*
> 1 PETER 1:6–7, NLT

These trials are only to test your faith, to show that it is strong and pure. It is being tested as fire tests and purifies gold—and your faith is far more precious to God than mere gold. So if your faith remains strong after fiery trials, it will bring you much praise and glory and honor on the day when Jesus Christ is revealed to the whole world.

One of the ways God answered my prayers was as follows: A fellow teacher persuaded me to attend a support group for family members of substance abusers. As I listened to the tragic stories about the pain that addicts had inflicted upon their families, I made an important decision: Danny was either going to get help or he was going to pack his bags. I knew I couldn't live through the experiences that these families had endured. My husband was a sick man, and while I had promised to love him in sickness and in health, I knew that allowing him to continue abusing his body was only harming him. I was giving him no reason to want to change.

I searched the Scripture for answers. I read 1 Corinthians 4:13, the verse stating that a believing woman must not divorce her unbelieving husband. Though Danny had at one time claimed to be a believer, he now rejected God and His Word and was living as an unbeliever. Was I supposed to stay in this marriage living on the hope that he might again draw close to the Lord and reclaim his salvation? Through much prayer and counsel, I decided that the best plan of action was to approach Danny in love about his salvation and his drinking problem.

When I confronted Danny, he adamantly denied having a problem. He flatly refused to get any help at all. I went back to the Word. This time God clearly spoke to me: "God has called us to live in peace" (1 Corinthians 7:15). There was my answer! There was no peace in my house. I wasn't ready to divorce Danny, but I knew that for sanity's sake, the baby and I must leave. We had to take care of ourselves in order to motivate Danny to take care of himself. Only then could we examine the future of our marriage.

I packed our things and explained to Danny, clearly and calmly, why I was leaving. I told him we would return if he dealt with his addiction—that until then, we had to live apart.

I took the baby and went to live with my parents. Danny was stunned. He showed up at the door, begging me to return; I refused. Desperate, he attended church one Sunday and sat with me. I told him that church attendance wasn't enough, and he agreed to begin counseling with our minister.

We spent more than two hours in the pastor's study the next week, where Danny tried to convince us both that he didn't have a problem. I felt so hopeless when I left that day. But I kept my resolution—I refused to move home or to even answer Danny's calls.

Every Sunday he came to church and took his seat beside me. At the end of the month, he went forward to accept Jesus. Danny promised me that he would change his behavior, but when I told him he had to give up drinking and drugs before I would return, he became angry and stopped calling me. I was so frightened—was our marriage really over? I continued to pray. Less than thirty days after he had accepted the Lord, Danny entered a substance abuse treatment center.

For the first time in months I felt hope, but my support group told me not to let my guard down until Danny had completed his treatment. When the pastor called to ask if I would attend a family weekend at the rehabilitation center, I agreed; there I found my husband a broken man, fully acknowledging his problems and willing to walk in sobriety.

When Danny left the treatment center, he was still the fun-loving guy I had fallen in love with, but he had matured in both mind and spirit. I packed my bags and returned home. Danny completely turned his life around, and I am happy to tell you today that God healed and restored our family. Thanks be to God that He heard my prayers and gave me strength to take the steps necessary to save my family. As His Word promised, wonderful joy lay ahead!

This woman took a completely different, God-guided approach to redeeming her marriage: She removed herself from the problem so that her husband could see it for himself. And he did! This woman proved Proverbs 12:4 to be true: "A wife of noble character is her husband's crown, but a disgraceful wife is like decay in his bones." She was truly her husband's crown.

Take each other for better or worse but not for granted.
ARLENE DAHL

BUILDING A MAN WITH YOUR HANDS

When God created man from the dust of the earth and woman from the rib of man and brought them together, He entrusted us with an awesome responsibility: maintaining a marital relationship. It is our duty as wives to build up our husbands and our homes. Fortunately, God never leaves us helpless in the face of this amazing assignment, but provides the power we need if we will allow Him to do so.

My friend Beth knew this truth, but she let it slip through her fingers when the unemployment storms blew her husband's business away. She lost confidence in him and in the Lord and chose instead to build her own house, leaving her husband tossing in the wind. Beth's story illustrates the importance of setting priorities when women choose to have careers. The same is true for men. Here is the story in her own words.

When my husband's business failed, I panicked. Instead of encouraging him in the midst of the storm, I decided to calm the winds with my own hands. I studied for my real estate license and returned to the workforce in an effort to help financially. I had some excellent contacts in the community and through our church, and I became an overnight success.

A year later my husband found another job, but he was earning far less money than before. "Beth, you can quit your job now," he told me at the end of the year. "I can take care of things."

"We can't possibly live on what you are making!" I replied indignantly.

"If we cut back in certain areas, I'm sure we can," he said.

"The children are older and don't need me at home during the day, and you have to agree that the extra income is nice."

"It's nice all right, but I'd rather have my wife at home," Greg replied.

"Well, I love working, and I love all the extra things that my money can buy for the house. The children aren't complaining either—Jenny has her piano lessons, and June has the best math tutor that money can buy."

My husband's shoulders sagged. I chose to ignore his plea, believing stubbornly that I was helping to ease the financial burden.

Suddenly, my job began to consume me. I found myself working every weekend and most weeknights, so I was not at home to see that my husband's self-esteem was plummeting. Every time he tried to talk to me, I was interrupted by a phone call about a house I had listed. When he protested, I snapped that he was interfering with my work.

Months passed and on my birthday, I complained that we hadn't been intimate in weeks and I wanted to make love that night.

"I'm sorry," my husband said quietly. "I just don't feel up to it."

We had a king-size bed and that night we slept what felt like miles apart. He ignored every effort I made to reach for him. I didn't like what was happening to my marriage.

The next morning at breakfast I told Greg that we needed to talk. "I've been trying to talk to you for months," he said sadly. Our oldest daughter, Jenny, joined us at the breakfast table just as the words left my husband's mouth.

"I've been trying to talk to you, too, Mom," Jenny complained. "You're never home anymore."

"What is this?" I asked. "Gang-Up-On-Mom Day?"

"It's true," Greg agreed. "You're almost never around. Even when you are home, you're always on the phone."

"Dad's telling the truth, Mom," Jenny said. "You haven't been to a single one of my soccer games this year."

"Well, you certainly aren't complaining about all of your new clothes, Jenny," I retorted. She jumped up from the table and ran out the door in tears. I felt hurt, unappreciated, and unfairly attacked.

"Beth, I'd really like for you to quit your job," Greg said.

On the verge of tears, I promised Greg that I would cut back. But every day my business grew, and I found it impossible to say no to a new client. The very next Sunday a big client came to town, and

I had to miss church. I felt a twinge of guilt as I watched my two teenagers leave for the service with their father, but I justified my absence when I sold a house later that day.

One evening when I returned home late from the office, my husband was waiting for me in the den.

"I need to talk to you, Beth," he said. "Things aren't going well at my job."

"Can it wait, Greg?" I asked. "I'm exhausted."

He stood up and went to bed without a word. Again, we slept miles apart.

The next morning I attempted to make amends. "Tell me what's bothering you at work, Greg."

"It's not that important," he said.

I answered him defensively. "Have it your way."

"Do you really care?" he asked.

"Of course I care; don't act like such a baby. Tell me what you wanted to tell me last night."

"I wanted to tell you that I was just passed over for a promotion—" The phone interrupted him. It was my client, and I became engrossed in conversation. I scarcely noticed that Greg had left when I rushed off to the office to make yet another sale.

The next Sunday morning at the breakfast table I told the family I couldn't go to church again. "Cancel your appointment and come with us," Greg urged me.

"But I can't. These are out-of-town clients."

"Can't they wait just a couple of hours for you?" he pleaded.

"They have to find a house before they return to Chicago. Every minute counts," I told him. "Besides, you just told me you've been passed over for a promotion. Your job might not even be secure. Where would we be if I weren't working and you got fired?"

Greg hung his head, but I was too busy to dwell on it. I came home late for dinner that night with what I thought was a good excuse. I had made a sale before my clients left for Chicago. My family was still sulking, and again I felt unappreciated.

"Beth, don't forget next Saturday night," Greg reminded me. "I've invited my boss to dinner."

Saturday night came—and guess what? I forgot to take the flank steak out of the freezer. We had to take his boss out to dinner. Greg's disappointment was palpable.

I felt defensive—I was helping the family, after all! I didn't deserve all this resentment. I put the incident out of my mind. And Greg and I went to bed another night without speaking.

Later in the week I went over to the home of an elderly woman whom I knew from church. Her husband had died several months before, and she wanted to put her house on the market. As I walked through the rooms with Mrs. Jenkins, she happily began to recall the years she had spent with her husband. Something began to stir within me, something more powerful than guilt. It was conviction. It cut to the core when Mrs. Jenkins also spoke of regretting that she had not relished every precious moment with her husband while he was alive.

When we sat down to the paperwork, Mrs. Jenkins looked me straight in the eye and said, "Beth, you haven't been to church for a while. You dropped out of our Bible study a year ago. We've been praying for you, dear, but I'm concerned that you are moving further and further from the Lord."

Mrs. Jenkins' words stung me. I looked down at the table.

"How are you being fed these days?" she asked.

I had to admit that not only was I starving spiritually, but I was also not feeding my family emotionally or spiritually, either. My confession spilled out. For the first time in months I looked at where I was and at what my family had been telling me. It wasn't pretty.

Mrs. Jenkins listened patiently. Then she asked in her direct but gentle manner, "What are you going to do about it, Beth?"

I stared at her blankly. I didn't know how to regain the ground I'd lost. I felt clueless.

"I would give anything to go back and spend just one more hour with my husband," Mrs. Jenkins said sadly. "Go home, Beth. Make restitution now, before it's too late."

When I returned home, my husband and daughters were asleep. I stayed up for two hours, pacing the floor. Finally I sat down in the den, opened my Bible, and began to read. The Lord spoke clearly to me: "Do not store up for yourselves treasures on earth, where moth and rust destroy, and where thieves break in and steal. But store up for yourselves treasures in heaven, where moth and rust do not destroy, and where thieves do not break in and steal. For where your treasure is, there your heart will be also" (Matthew 6:19–21).

I realized with sadness that my heart was not right with my husband, with my daughters, or with Jesus—I had stored up meaningless treasures in my work. The money, prestige, and success weren't enough to counterbalance my emptiness. I went to bed and cried myself to sleep.

The next morning I called my family to the breakfast table. For the first time in months I didn't serve cold cereal; I had eggs, bacon, and toast awaiting them.

"Mom, you haven't cooked breakfast in over a year," said June, visibly surprised.

"What's the special occasion?" Jenny asked.

"Mom's coming home," I said with a smile. I could hardly believe that I had spoken those words.

Greg searched my face. The girls were smiling.

"I'm going in today to resign," I announced. "We might have to tighten our belts a bit."

"That won't be necessary," Greg said. "I am up for another promotion."

"A promotion!" I exclaimed. "Why didn't you tell me?"

"I tried to tell you several times, but you were too busy to listen."

"Well, I'm not too busy now," I said resolutely. "Why don't you tell us about it?"

Greg beamed as he spoke about applying for a position as sales manager. "It may take a few months, but with commissions I could be earning as much as I used to," he said proudly.

"In the meantime, I'll get a baby-sitting job, Mom," June volunteered. My eyes brimmed with tears.

"I don't need those piano lessons anymore, Mom," Jenny volunteered. "I don't even like playing the piano anyway." I hugged my daughters.

"With your encouragement," Greg told me, "I believe that I can get that job, Beth."

Greg's words stung me. Had he been passed over for the last promotion due to a lack of confidence? I realized that I hadn't been around to lend the support that my husband had needed. I was not going to let that happen again.

Later that day I went into the office to resign. My broker tried to convince me to stay—to cut back, not to quit. But I knew what I had to do, and I made certain she was aware that my decision was final. That night Greg and I made love for the first time in months.

The next morning I surprised my friends by showing up at Bible study. I hugged Mrs. Jenkins. "I've turned your listing over to another agent in the office," I confided. "I'm certain that she'll do a fine job for you."

"I'm not worried a bit," Mrs. Jenkins replied. "And I couldn't be happier for you."

The Scripture that our leader taught on that day was wonderfully appropriate: "The wise woman builds her house, but with her own hands the foolish one tears hers down" (Proverbs 14:1). I had torn down my house—my relationship with my husband and my children, the support I had once given them—and everyone had paid for my mistake. I longed to rebuild our family, and I committed to it that very day.

To be perfectly honest, it took some adjusting to become a mom, a wife, and a daughter of the *King* again, but I was faithful. Over the next few months I saw God restore every area of my life. I can truly say today that the treasures of my heart reside in love for my children, my husband, and my Lord.

With my encouragement and nurturing, Greg excelled within the new company and was soon promoted to sales manager. By the next year he was running the entire company.

When our girls left for college, Greg suggested that I go back to real estate if I found myself bored at home.

"Bored with you?" I laughed. "Never!" All of the empty places in my heart were overflowing with love that I had rediscovered for my family through Jesus. I would never again be empty.

If you treat a man as he is,
He'll stay as he is,
But if you treat him as if he were
What he ought to be, and could be,
He will become the bigger and better man.

GOETHE

PROMISES TO STAND ON

Promise: God grows the seeds we plant. "It is not that we think we can do anything of lasting value by ourselves. Our only power and success comes from God" (2 Corinthians 3:5, NLT).

In the midst of a marital storm, you may long for sunshine. Instant change happens rarely—in most situations, growth occurs gradually. But while you wait, you can be taking action, giving God seeds that He can nurture into fruitful vines of marital harmony. As my friend Beth discovered, and as the writer of Proverbs pointed out, "The wise woman builds her house, but with her own hands the foolish one tears hers down" (Proverbs 14:1). Here are some love potions that go a long way toward building a loving household. I realize that not all of you will be able to use these. Some of you wish that your husband would make the first move—you feel that it's his turn to improve things between the two of you. Let's face it: You can't change anyone but you. And you are responsible to do all the good you can. Even if you feel reluctant, try one or two of these suggestions. See how your husband responds—you may be surprised!

• *Create a shelter from the storms of life.* My mother was a master at creating a home that exuded love and acceptance. She designated a special chair for my father and guarded his solitude when he needed it. Do the same for your husband: Give him a seat of honor and space to reflect. He will love you for this!

• *Transform your bedroom into the Garden of Eden.* Put a lock on your bedroom door so that the two of you can enjoy privacy. Add some romantic touches—soft new sheets with a thread count above 280, plump pillows, and a down comforter. Install dimmers on your overhead lights. To create a romantic environment, light scented candles and place a bouquet of fresh flowers and a bowl of fragrant potpourri in the room. Buy an inexpensive compact disc player and play romantic, soothing music. Toss that ratty underwear and invest in some pretty lingerie. Make the room inviting—then invite him in!

• *Praise him regularly.* Praise your heavenly Father for your husband, but praise your husband as well. "Pleasant words are a honeycomb, sweet to the soul and healing to the bones" (Proverbs 16:24). Find a small cardboard box. Cut out thirty paper hearts. On each, write one thing about which to praise your husband. Each morning pull out a heart, and praise your husband for that quality several times throughout the day. Recently I pulled out a heart that read, *Praise Ken for his nice legs*. Let me tell you, Ken wore shorts around the house for the duration of the week. When we dressed to attend a black-tie event one evening, I was afraid that he was going to wear shorts with his tux! After you have gone through your thirty hearts, use them again or create some new ones.

• *Make a point of pleasing his palate.* Cook his favorite meals and special treats. Even after an exhausting day, when all I can do is pop a frozen dinner into the microwave, I still attempt to create a special atmosphere by adding a salad to the meal and some flowers to the table. My husband appreciates these special touches.

• *Attend his pity parties.* A little encouragement goes a long way! Recently, my husband was devastated over a business deal that had not worked out. His shoulders began to sag, and a deep furrow developed on his brow. He was hurting. In response, I listened every time he wanted to talk it through. And I tried to make the conversation move in a positive direction: I began to reflect on his past accomplishments and on his future. Instead of focusing on what he should have done, of which I have been guilty in the past, I assured him that I stood by him in every decision. I mentally put on my old cheerleading uniform, grabbed my pom-poms, and cheered him through the disappointment phase. And I let his close friends know that he needed love and encouragement. In short, I became a beacon of hope in my husband's storm.

• *Pray together to stay together.* Pray together over the problems you face—especially your marital problems. Relinquish your pain to God and ask Him to make beauty out of conflict. Do not use the opportunity to list the ways in which he needs to improve. Instead, thank God for how hard your husband is trying or for some small victory you've witnessed together. Ask God to convict you about ways in which you may be hurting the relationship. Pray together at least once a day about all of your concerns and praise God for all of your blessings.

• *Stand on the promises as a couple.* "Whoever gives heed to instruction prospers, and blessed is he who trusts in the LORD" (Proverbs 16:20). Schedule a devotional time together and search the Word for God's promises. Anytime you feel you are sinking in the storm, read the Scriptures aloud. Test them. Seek the Lord together; He provides a uniquely powerful glue for relationships.

After marriage, all things change. And one of them better be you.

ELIZABETH HAWES

Promise: We will reap good things—if we sow them. "Do not be deceived: God cannot be mocked. A man reaps what he sows. The one who sows to please his sinful nature, from that nature will reap destruction; the one who sows to please the Spirit, from the Spirit will reap eternal life. Let us not become weary in doing good, for at the proper time we will reap a harvest if we do not give up" (Galatians 6:7–9).

Has the road to marital peace seemed too long already? Are you tired of trying, sick of hoping, finding yourself speechless at prayer time? Friend, don't give up now. Wait for the Lord to finish the work He has begun. Let Him create a harvest.

Do you need fresh ideas? Here are some seeds worth sowing:

• *Godly, well-timed advice.* God blessed woman with her own perspective so that she could gently advise her husband. The wife has a special sensitivity that allows her to see things that her husband cannot see. The key, however, is to do so only at the Lord's leading. You will discern these things over time through prayer. Recently Ken was about to enter a business deal with a man whom I sensed was not honorable. I prayerfully considered telling Ken of my strong feelings; one evening I felt God's release to do so. Sure enough, the man was later proven dishonest. This is a very sensitive arena, though—you have to earn your husband's trust before you earn the right to advise him. Pursue the Lord and His wisdom, letting your actions speak for you. As your husband comes to rely upon your good character and clarity of mind, you will become an invaluable helpmate.

• *Appointments for resolution.* "There is a time for everything, and a season for every activity under heaven...a time to be silent and a time to speak" (Ecclesiastes 3:1, 7). Don't bombard your husband with problems when he walks in the door at the end of the day. Be savvy about when to speak and when to keep silent. Ken and I have found it helpful to make appointments for discussing unpleasantness. Set aside a time each week to talk over your problems. If you have an emergency, use as much tact and gentleness as you can if the time is not ideal.

• *Fair fighting techniques.* Do not attack, bring up the past, or loosely use the words *you, always,* and *never.* Do inject some humor (if you can), postpone arguments when you're on your way to a social event or business appointment, agree to disagree at bedtime, and use kisses and prayers generously. "A gentle answer turns away wrath, but a harsh word stirs up anger" (Proverbs 15:1). Instead of accusing each other, discuss your feelings. If things get really heated, take a time-out and resume your discussion later. You may forget what you were arguing about! A godly counselor gave Ken and me some great advice: During an argument, get an index card to pass back and forth. The person with the card is allowed to speak without interruption. If necessary, clock the time you spend holding the card, and take turns speaking. It works—I know!

• *Apologies at the ready.* "I'm sorry" should be frequently used words in your vocabulary. When you live with someone, everyday offenses happen. We are all selfish at times and should always be ready with "I'm sorry" when we hurt our mate. Often we have to say it even when we don't feel it. Say the words with your mouth, and allow God to bring them to pass in your heart. "The tongue that brings healing is a tree of life" (Proverbs 15:4).

• *Walks down memory lane.* Look back at how you met, and refresh the feelings of those early love-filled days to remember why you got married in the first place. When you recount the difficulties you have walked through since, you gain confidence to face the trials that are ahead. In the same way that reflecting on your Christian journey and the miracles God has done in your life helps build your faith for the future, revisiting His faithfulness in your marriage helps you trust Him completely in the midst of the storm. "May your fountain be blessed, and may you rejoice in the wife of your youth" (Proverbs 5:18).

• *Thirty-second hugs.* This love prescription is guaranteed to bring healing to your marriage. Make a personal pledge to give your husband a thirty-second hug every morning and night. Nothing is more comforting than being held in the arms of the one you love. You may not realize how short thirty seconds is! When you and your husband embrace, you will often find the anger, the hurt, the resentment, and the fear falling away like leaves descending from trees. The thirty-second hug can work miracles. Try it!

Often the difference between a successful marriage and a mediocre one consists of leaving about three or four things a day unsaid.

HARLAN MILLER

Promise: Forgiveness begets forgiveness. "Blessed are the merciful, for they will be shown mercy" (Matthew 5:7). When you're struggling through a marital storm and blame flies around in every conversation, forgiveness may be the last thing on your mind. But forgiving your mate is more than a good idea—it is a key to forgiving ourselves.

Jesus was very blunt about this. "If you forgive men when they sin against you, your heavenly Father will also forgive you. But if you do not forgive men their sins, your Father will not forgive your sins" (Matthew 6:14–15). It is in showing mercy that we also receive mercy.

Does forgiving mean that you give up trying to fix what is wrong in the relationship? No, but it means that you start fresh each day. It means that you wipe clean your husband's record and seek forgiveness for your own record. It means that you make mercy central in your relationship. Remember the quote that started this chapter— "A happy marriage is the union of two forgivers"? Doesn't that make sense?

Fuller Seminary theologian Dr. Lewis Smedes wrote, "Forgiving is a gift God has given us for healing ourselves before we are ready to help anyone else." He also noted, "Forgiving our enemy does not necessarily turn him into a close friend or a promising husband or a trustworthy partner."

I have discovered that it does, however, mend the fracture our damaged emotions have incurred inside. And it clears the way for relational mending as well. Smedes goes on to say, "We do not diminish the wrongness of what he did to us. We do not blind ourselves to the reality that he is perfectly capable of doing it again. But we take him back into our private world as a person who shares our faulty humanity, bruised like us, faulty like us, still thoroughly blamable for what he did to us. Yet, human like us."[1]

In other words, when we can accept each other as mere mortals, we begin to heal our relationship. We also make room for God. He told the apostle Paul: "I am with you; that is all you need. My power shows up best in weak people" (2 Corinthians 12:9, TLB).

Isn't that comforting? My weakness creates an opportunity for God to act. Friend, invite Him into your storm. Let Him guide you down paths of forgiveness—for your husband's sake, as well as for your own. See where mercy takes you. It is certain to be a good place.

CONCLUSION: WATCH FOR A CHANGE IN THE CLOUDS

Storms blow in, but eventually they break. Where are you in your marital storm today? In the early stages, with the raindrops just beginning to fall and the winds having only slightly picked up? In the eye, where a deceptive calm is trying to persuade you that the raging storm does not really exist? Or in the aftermath, surveying the havoc wreaked by years of damage with no end in sight?

Wherever you are, know that storms—while a very real part of life—are also temporal. The earth couldn't withstand being pelted indefinitely by nature's fury; in the same way, humans cannot withstand endless turmoil. How will you know when your storm is about to break? *Don't go it alone.* Get under the umbrella of a trusted Christian counselor who can offer a lifeline between God and you, who can help support you as you endure. A change is coming.

Consider my friends Judy and Jerry Schreur. Their love story is a modern one: When they married, Jerry appeared not on a white horse but on a motorcycle to sweep young Judy off her feet. She was eighteen and pregnant; he was an unemployed convicted felon. Talk about the future looking dim! Is love blind, or what? Two years and two babies later, in a drafty house that was falling apart, with no money and little communication, Judy's eyes were opened, and she began to wonder about her prince. Their dark and stormy marriage looked bleak.

Three decades later they are still together—happily—and share ministry, laughter, and marital delight. The answer? The stormbreaker? God Himself. Someone introduced the Schreurs to Jesus, and in Him they found the glue to mend all of the cracks in their relationship. Sure, they still have their bad moments and disagreements—what couple doesn't? But they know they are stuck together. And they enjoy it!

Friend, your storm is bound to have a break. Watch for it, pray for it. And let God give you hope today.

There is nothing more lovely in life than the union of two people
whose love for one another has grown through the years
from the small acorn of passion to a great rooted tree.
Surviving all vicissitudes, and rich with its manifold branches,
every leaf holding its own significance.

VITA SACKVILLE-WEST

CHAPTER THREE

EMPTY ARMS, EMPTY CRIB

Hope. . .is not a feeling; it is something you do.
KATHERINE PATERSON

For those of you who desperately yearn for children, infertility issues and miscarriages deliver some of life's most devastating blows. The experience of childlessness is especially searing in a world full of young people. You can't do anything—go to dinner and a movie, attend a church service, shop—without encountering a child or an expecting mother. Baby-shower invitations, parenting magazine offers, and free samples of "kid-tested" laundry detergent litter your mailbox. Commercials hyping the "coolest" toys blare from your television. And then there's the painful tug you feel inside—quiet, persistent, relentless.

This is a storm of stinging winds and cold, pelting rain. It is a haunting pain, often long lasting. It is very lonely. The childless woman feels singled out: Why does *everyone's* womb but hers work? We often observe couples that would make wonderful parents finding themselves infertile, while other women are unable to care for their children.

Let us start by admitting that this is a mystery as well as a storm. And although we cannot necessarily understand it, we can endure it. How? By moving from the shifting sands of our dreams to the solid rock of God's promises. We can't exist for long on our desire; we *can* stand forever on God's faithfulness.

GOD WILL NOT LEAVE YOU WANTING

Key Promise: "Don't be impatient. Wait for the Lord, and he will come and save you! Be brave, stouthearted and courageous. Yes, wait and he will help you" (Psalm 27:14, TLB).

My friend Diane Waggoner shared her thoughts about the pain of infertility. Perhaps she speaks for you:

Infertility is hard because it starts with *in*—just like the words *inadequate, inferior,* and *incapable.*

Infertility is hard because when your period appears each month, hope disappears.

Infertility is hard because sex is scheduled by ovulation, not by passion and desire.

Infertility is hard because the fertility medication makes you fat, grouchy, and gives you migraines, but it doesn't always make you a mother or give you babies.

Infertility is hard because Satan whispers, "It's because you would be a bad mother and God doesn't trust you with children."

Infertility is hard because the Bible says, "Children are a gift of the Lord…. Blessed is the man whose quiver is full of them" (Psalm 127:3, 5, NASB), and you wonder if your husband can truly be happy with an empty quiver.

Infertility is hard because even though you blow out all the candles on your birthday cake, wishes do not always come true.

This is a subject that has broken hearts and inflicted pain since the beginning of time. This primal human hurt is also something we can take to God, something for which we can ask His touch, help, and healing. While infertility is a storm I have not encountered, it is one I have witnessed in the lives of numerous dear friends. I have spied the silent tears, hugged the young woman who has wistful eyes, counseled the grieving about the children that never came. I have also waited in hope, prayed with passion, and witnessed God's astonishing ability to do what we can't. He is faithful, friend, and He will not leave His beloved children wanting.

Let me be clear here: I believe that our heavenly Father will fulfill every desire. King David declared that when he said, "The LORD is my shepherd, I shall not be in want" (Psalm 23:1). Does this mean that every longing mother will someday hold a child of her own? That every closed womb will eventually produce? That those empty arms will be filled? The Word of God does not promise any of these things. What God does tell us is that He will not allow pain to consume and defeat us. God invites us to share our pain with Him and then let Him work with it—stand on His promises and watch His plan unfold. The result, I assure you, will be beautiful.

As with all other storms, God's Word and His faithfulness are equal to the challenge. He gives us certainties for our comfort and a hope upon which we can feast. The Bible illustrates a powerful example in the story of Zechariah, a priest, and his wife, Elizabeth: "Both of them were upright in the sight of God, observing all the Lord's commandments and regulations blamelessly" (Luke 1:6). The next verse reveals a very human side to these righteous people: "But they had no children, because Elizabeth was barren; and they were both well along in years."

Like me, do you immediately sense the pain behind those words? Do you suspect that Elizabeth and Zechariah occasionally thought, *The Lord is good, and ministry is wonderful, but I wish...?*

Don't you imagine that as a young couple they dreamed of children, grandchildren, perhaps even great-grandchildren to bounce on their knees?

The Bible confirms our suspicions. One day when Zechariah was going about his work, burning incense in the Lord's temple, an angel appeared to him and said, "Do not be afraid, Zechariah; your prayer has been heard. Your wife Elizabeth will bear you a son, and you are to give him the name John. He will be a joy and delight to you, and many will rejoice because of his birth" (Luke 1:13–14).

Apparently the news was just too good, because Zechariah decided to argue with the angel. He reminded Gabriel that he and Elizabeth were very old. (Perhaps the aged priest didn't trust his own senses—who would, under the circumstances?) He asked for a sign, and he received one. "You will be silent and not able to speak until the day this happens, because you did not believe my words, which will come true at their proper time" (v. 20). Let this be a lesson to us: Do not resist God's promises!

Sure enough, Zechariah lost his voice, and Elizabeth gained weight—due to pregnancy, of course. When she delivered a son, her praise was simple, straightforward, and heartfelt: "'The Lord has done this for me,' she said. 'In these days he has shown his favor and taken away my disgrace among the people'" (v. 25). We see later in Luke's Gospel that Gabriel used Elizabeth's example to show Jesus' mother, Mary, what God could do: "Even Elizabeth your relative is going to have a child in her old age, and she who was said to be barren is in her sixth month. For nothing is impossible with God" (vv. 36–37).

We can draw several truths from this story. First, of course, the angel's statement: "Nothing is impossible with God." But let's not stop there. Though we see clearly that God is the giver of life, the opener of the womb, we do not see any promises that God plans to give every woman the gift he gave Elizabeth. Her pregnancy, you see, served several purposes. Yes, it gave her great joy, but it also fulfilled part of God's ultimate plan—a beautiful strategy of salvation for mankind. And it served as instruction to young Mary, who was about to enter her own uniquely frightening ordeal.

Friend, I want Luke 1:37 to be of great encouragement to you if you are trying to conceive. It is true that God gave this wonderful word to a woman in your very situation—he promised a child in the midst of barrenness! But I also want you to keep your heart open to the other purposes God may want to fulfill through you. As a disciple of Jesus, you play a pivotal role in God's plan to redeem the world. And every detail, even the heartbreak of infertility, can represent a piece of the puzzle.

What God does promise is *help*. The ache you feel for a child will not always define you; the pain will not always darken long days. I believe in and have seen our key promise at work: "Wait for the Lord, and he will come and save you! Be brave, stouthearted and courageous. Yes, wait and he will help you" (Psalm 27:14, TLB). Either you will be given a child, or that raging desire will cease. Remember how Jesus instructed us to seek first His kingdom (Matthew 6:33)? Do you recall how David told us to delight ourselves in our Father (Psalm 37:4)? As we obey these commands, our wills blend with His. If His perfect plan includes children, they will come—nothing can stop them! If His plan does not, we will find that longing lifted. It *is* that simple.

If you are in the midst of this very bitter storm, you may be assured that God offers protection. You don't have to be crippled by a sick heart; reach out for His promise of help and cling to it, and wait and see what God can do! I do not know what the outcome will be, but I do know that you can trust in the One who does.

The following stories illustrate how several couples stood on God's promises. In several cases the result was not what they had hoped for, but there is one constant throughout: the couples' claim,

"I would have gone through it all again just to be where I am today." Now that's a comfort!

Come meet these friends who discovered firm ground in God's promises.

Desire is prayer.
TERRY MCMILLAN

GREAT NEWS: IT AIN'T OVER TILL IT'S OVER!

Meet my friend Sheri, who thought she knew what God had planned for her. I first met Sheri Rose Shepherd, former Mrs. America, at a bookseller's convention in Nashville. Ken had told me Sheri's fascinating life story: Once an overweight, insecure, drug- and food-addicted young woman, Sheri was totally transformed when she met Jesus. Ken had told me to be sure to introduce myself to Sheri, her husband, Steve, and their son, Jacob, when I arrived in Nashville.

We hit it off instantly! Sheri had scheduled a conference in the Nashville area apart from the booksellers' convention and had invited my friend Ann Platz and me to attend. We were excited for the opportunity to hear this beautiful, dynamic Christian speaker.

Along with hundreds of women, I was deeply moved by Sheri Rose's testimony and her teaching. But as I was sitting in the audience, for some reason I kept picturing Sheri with a little girl. In my mind's eye I saw her next to a blue-eyed, blond youngster decked out in frilly clothes, ribbons, and a hat. I sensed that Sheri was the type of woman born to mother a little girl. I could tell she oozed with femininity—that she loved clothes, makeup, hair, and dolls. After the conference I casually asked Sheri if she had ever thought about having another child.

She threw me a horrified look—you know, the kind of look that says, "You've said the wrong thing; kindly remove the foot from your mouth and back away." Her eyes began to well with tears.

"Oh, please forgive me, Sheri," I said, aghast.

"No, no," she insisted. "It is just such a painful subject for me. I've wanted more children so badly, especially a girl." She confessed that the pursuit of another child had almost destroyed her. After enduring several miscarriages, she decided she couldn't take the pain and disappointment anymore. She had totally relinquished the desires of her heart and her husband had undergone a vasectomy only a few weeks before. "I won't ever have the little girl I longed for," she sighed.

Was I ever sorry that I had mentioned a baby girl! After drying her eyes, Sheri was very gracious about the situation. I thought that I might be able to lighten the mood; when we got back to the hotel I decided we should have a girls' night out. Sheri, Ann, my friend Susan Stafford, and I went out to a restaurant.

As we ate dinner, Sheri began to experience some nausea. "I'm not feeling very well," she said slowly.

I don't know what got into me that day. I immediately cried, "You're pregnant! I feel it in my spirit. I've been feeling it all day." The words just popped out—I couldn't help it. Ann and Susan looked at me as though I had lost my mind, especially since Ann had been present to witness my *faux pas* earlier that afternoon.

"But, Susan, that's impossible! I told you that Steve has had a vasectomy. Unless, of course…" She paused, then continued slowly, "I suppose it's possible that I could have gotten pregnant before Steve's surgery, but that's so unlikely."

Nausea was clearly upsetting her and I encouraged her to go to bed. I couldn't explain it, but I knew Sheri Rose was pregnant. So I promised, "I'll bring you a pregnancy test in the morning."

Ann and I drove all over Nashville trying to find a drugstore open at six in the morning. We finally spotted a twenty-four-hour K-Mart. I rushed in and bought two pregnancy tests. (I knew it would take more than one to convince Sheri Rose that she was pregnant.)

Back at the hotel, I knocked on the Shepherds' hotel room door. The whole family greeted me, and I handed over the pregnancy tests. Then Ann and I left.

Later that morning Sheri Rose and her son Jacob, both grinning from ear to ear, showed up at our publisher's booth to announce that she was pregnant! She told us that on her way to the booth she had run into another dear friend and fellow author, Michelle McKinney Hammond, and had given her the wonderful news. Earlier that morning, Sheri and her husband discussed keeping the news a secret, since they had suffered three miscarriages, but they had decided to step out on faith. Upon hearing that Sheri was pregnant, and that she had had previous miscarriages, Michelle immediately laid her hands on Sheri's tummy and prayed for the baby's safe arrival into the world.

Don't ask me why, but Sheri's news didn't surprise me in the least. Poor Sheri was deathly ill with morning sickness almost the entire pregnancy, and received a real scare during the labor, when the doctor told her that the cord was wrapped around the baby's neck. Michelle's early prayer was definitely needed! Sheri gave birth to a darling baby girl, whom she named Emily Joy. And today Emily looks just the way I pictured her, a blond, blue-eyed cream puff who wears lots of bows and hats, decked out in frilly pink outfits. I know that God has a great plan for this child's life. Guess who is the baby's godmother and who prays for that plan daily?

Let me quickly add that visions are not my spiritual expertise. This was a highly unusual occurrence for me; it has never happened again. For some reason, I was allowed to be a part of God's plan for Sheri.

Sheri's story is an example of trust in God and refusal to give in to doubt or fear. She chose to stop flailing in the storm and put herself under the shelter of God's complete care. Trust transformed a miserable situation. Scripture tells us: "God opposes the proud but gives grace to the humble. Humble yourselves, therefore, under God's mighty hand, that he may lift you up in due time" (1 Peter 5:5–6). "He guides the humble in what is right and teaches them his way" (Psalm 25:9). Relinquishment and submission invite God's perfect intervention; they create room for miracles. Discover the lovely gift, as Sheri did, of letting go.

> *The grand essentials to happiness in this life are something to do, something to love, and something to hope for.*
>
> JOSEPH ADDISON

SPECIAL DELIVERY

My friend Bill Jensen provided an incredible blessing when he suggested that I invite Marsha Mark to share about the storm of infertility that she and her husband endured for over six years. Marsha tells the following story, along with other extraordinary stories from her life in her new book *101 Amazing Things about God* (River Oak Publishing Company, Fall 2001).

After six years, Marsha's doctor told her and her husband that they needed to accept that they would never have biological children. The state agency had turned down their repeated adoption requests due to age; and financially, a private adoption was out of the question.

Amidst the storm clouds, a friend gave Marsha some encouraging words. "I don't know how, Marsha, but God is going to use your struggle with infertility for His glory." Marsha began to pray for a glimpse of that glory.

Marsha tells her own story:

For six months I'd been praying earnestly. I'd asked everyone I knew, and even some I didn't know at all, to pray…that somehow, if it be God's will, my husband, Tom, and I would be able to have a baby.

The most precious prayers were offered by little children. One five-year-old prayer warrior friend gave God suggestions: "Dear God, please send Marsha a baby. Maybe someone could give her one, or she could just find one on the street. Thank You. Amen."

My husband didn't pray. He'd stopped praying after the last specialist told him all the reasons I'd never conceive. He'd stopped praying after the last adoption agency turned us down. He'd stopped praying after he realized the cost of a private adoption. And he'd stopped praying when he realized that I was in full-blown menopause.

Being a scientist, Tom had seen all the facts. And in his lifetime, he'd never seen prayer change facts.

As I reread the *Christian Reader* article I'd written six months before, I suddenly didn't feel well. Something wasn't right.

Maybe you have cancer, the hypochondriac in me taunted.

I made an appointment at the infertility clinic. I told them my concerns and asked for some tests—including one more pregnancy test. They looked at me with pity in their eyes and said gently but firmly, "No."

"The doctor has shown you your hormone count. You haven't had any cycles for seven months because you are in menopause. Asking for another pregnancy test only indicates that you are not accepting things as they are."

Although they didn't come out and say it, they implied that I needed a therapist to help me deal with my infertility.

I begged for the extra test; they resisted.

Finally, I convinced them. But they weren't going to rush the test through while I was there. Why bother?

The next day at home, the phone rang.

"Marsha, your pregnancy test came back positive."

"For what?" I said. *Maybe there's some new type of cancer that only shows up on a positive pregnancy test,* I thought to myself.

"For pregnancy."

"What!?!"

After the sixth repetition, I said, "Could you hold for a minute? I'd like to get my husband on the phone."

With trembling fingers I speed-dialed a three-way call.

"Tom," I said, with an urgency in my voice, "I've got the hospital on the line. Nurse, could you please tell my husband what you've just told me?"

"Your wife's pregnancy test came back positive."

"For what?" Tom also wondered if something was wrong.

"For pregnancy. Your wife is pregnant."

With characteristic understatement, Tom said, "Well, that's interesting."

How is this possible?

The next day I went in for a sonogram. A heartbeat wasn't visible yet, but there was a yolk sac. From a blood test they determined I had conceived eleven days before. It was exactly the time for me to get supplemental progesterone to help the baby adhere to the wall—one of my problems in conceiving.

Over the next fourteen days, I had four more pregnancy tests and three more sonograms at the hospital's request. I think they were having trouble dealing with the facts.

The first time I saw the little heart beating I burst into tears.

My full-term pregnancy was uneventful—unless you count every day bathed in praise for the answer to our prayer. On October 22, 1996, Amanda Joy was born. We call her Miracle Mandy.

It's hard to imagine a child who was ever more loved or such a great boost to her daddy's belief in prayer.

In our kitchen, by the back door, there's a little imprint of Amanda Joy's feet when she was just a few months old. Underneath the imprint is a verse: "What is impossible with man is possible with God."

We often tell our little prayer warrior friend that God listened to—and took—a child's suggestion. We did find our baby on the street—the street of faith, paved with the prayers of believers.

Marsha's story is a perfect example of how God's strength makes up for our weakness. And how He, in His faithfulness, overlooks our lack!

> *If logic tells you that life is a meaningless accident,*
> *don't give up on life. Give up on logic.*
> SHIRA MILGROM

A BIGGER PLAN

"I have held my friends' babies in my arms, but I know now that I will never hold my own baby in my arms. I have put my hand on a friend's pregnant tummy, but I am never going to know what it feels like to feel a child move inside of me. I will never know the joy of seeing the first smile, the first step, or the first tooth." Today my friend Abby can speak these words without tears or anguish, but for more than twenty years she battled every infertility storm known to womankind.

Abby and her husband, Dan, tried everything—from praying to consulting the leading fertility experts. After spending thousands of dollars, they met nothing but defeat every step of the way. Yet for years their faith remained steady. "We stood on the promises of God without wavering," Abby says. "I must have repeated the Scripture 'All things work together for good to those who love God, to those who are the called according to His purpose' [Romans 8:28, NKJV] at least a thousand times a week. I believed that God's delay in answering our prayer was being used not only to teach us to trust Him, but also for His ultimate glory."

Ten long years inched by, and the baby never came. Finally this couple's faith was shaken. I'll let Abby tell the rest of the story.

Dan and I lapsed into anger against God. We had trusted Him with all our hearts and He had let us down! Bitterness seeped in from every direction, and one day as we looked into each other's eyes, we didn't like what we were becoming. "Let's get some help—now," Dan suggested.

Sitting with our pastor, we listened as he gave us a new Scripture to cling to: "Trust in the LORD with all your heart and lean not on your own understanding; in all your ways acknowledge him, and he will make your paths straight" (Proverbs 3:5–6). God's Word seemed to breathe life into us.

As we sat there sobbing, feeling God's presence, our pastor asked us, "Have you ever considered adoption?" We hadn't; Dan and I had focused solely on the infertility problem.

So after ten years we threw in the biological baby blanket and decided that we would adopt. Yet every attempt we made only stirred up disappointment. A friend suggested that we take in some foster children, both to help needy kids and to satisfy our longing for a family. We enthusiastically met with the agency and volunteered. As soon as all the red tape cleared, we became foster parents to two adorable toddlers: a three-year-old boy and his two-year-old sister. The kids adapted beautifully and seemed to bask in our love and parenting. We were a family!

After a couple of years, we were given the opportunity to adopt the children. God had heard our cries—we would be parents at last! But before we could begin the tedious adoption process, a social worker came to call. "I don't know quite how to tell you this," she said, "but the children's mother has been rehabilitated." Following a court date we sat humbly as a judge ruled that the mother was going to get her children back.

I just couldn't take it anymore. The old anger rose again. All I had ever dreamed of was being a wife and a mother. The reality of my situation left me feeling like half of a woman. And the disappointment of losing those two precious toddlers devastated me.

The day the agency took the children from us one of my friends drove me to her home in the mountains so I could get away. I spent two weeks alone with God. At this crossroad in my life I was forty-five years old, and for twenty of those years I'd been trying to become a mother. For the first ten years I had lived my life on a schedule of doctors' appointments, lovemaking sessions with my husband, and twenty-eight-day cycles. The second decade had been spent in the confusion of the adoption process. I realized that our mad pursuit for children had to end. Dan and I had tried everything and my arms were still empty. *What now, Lord?* I prayed. *I need answers! You told me not to lean on my own understanding and to trust You. I trusted You, and I still don't have a child. Lord, I've been begging for twenty years, and the crib is still empty! Why?*

For the next couple of days, I dredged myself in self-pity like a pig wallows in the mud. Why hadn't God given in to my demands? As I flipped through the Bible, He spoke to me through His Word. "He settles the barren woman in her home as a happy mother of children. Praise the LORD" (Psalm 113:9).

As I read these words, I felt an incredible peace wash over me. I stopped slumping in my chair and sat up straight. I needed to stop struggling, stop planning, stop fretting, and rest in God. I didn't feel God promising me a child so much as I felt Him renewing my spirit. I needed to accept that I might never be a mother, but that God still had a plan for my life! If I allowed Him to work in my heart, could I find happiness and fulfillment in this life even though my arms remained empty? I read the last words of the verse again: "Praise the LORD."

Suddenly, questions began pouring through my mind. I started to talk to the Lord. He asked, "Don't you have a wonderful husband?"

Of course! I responded. *Dan adores me—he treats me like a queen.*

"Just consider how many women would give their right arm to have a man like Dan love them."

Thank You, Lord, praise You for the gift of a loving and godly husband!

"What about health?"

Dan and I both enjoy radiant health! Thank You, Lord, that our bodies are wondrously made.

"Aren't you blessed with a wonderful family and a wide circle of friends who love you?"

Thank You, Lord, for my family and friends. They are a great blessing and an encouragement. My life is so full.

"Your life is full?"

Yes, my life is full and happy!

"Even without a baby? Children?"

Yes, Lord! I replied, with tears streaming down my face. *My life is full.* I began praising God with my whole heart for the life He had given me. I put praise music on the stereo and danced around the room.

I had arrived at my friend's farmhouse hurt, angry, and resentful, but when Dan came to meet me for the weekend, he discovered a new woman. "What in the world has happened to you?" he asked.

"Dan, God has given me an attitude of gratitude," I told him joyously. Over the next few days Dan joined me in praising God. When we walked out the door of the mountain cabin, we left our mutual desire for children behind.

At this very moment, as you are reading these words and longing for a child, your desire may be so intense that you probably cannot imagine how God could take the desire away. It is difficult to understand why He would refuse to bless us with children. Many times His ways transcend human logic, but we must trust Him and focus on our faith on Him, not on the circumstances. That's what Abby and Dan were able to do. They trusted God with all their hearts.

Did God answer their prayer? Did He eventually bless them with children? Not in the way they had originally hoped, but their maternal and paternal instincts were later fulfilled. Shortly after they returned from the cabin, Abby and Dan were asked to teach the youth group at their church. Since that pivotal day, hundreds of children have passed through their lives. Many of these children hungered for attention as well as love and affection. God placed Abby and Dan there to meet their needs.

Abby says today, "I've dressed more girls for proms, cheered at more ball games, and solved more young people's problems than I would have as a parent. Both Dan and I have become loving parents to so many children. Many of them had no love or help from their earthly parents, and God sent them to us for wisdom and healing. I couldn't love these kids any more if they were my flesh and blood.

"You know, had I been raising my own children, I would never have agreed to teach the youth group. God's plan for us was to influence hundreds of lives, not just the lives of the children I had hoped to have."

What an amazing story! You see, you *will* know God's provision—either His provision of a family or His provision of grace in the absence of a family. Expect to see Him act.

Be not hot in prayer and cold in praise.

ANONYMOUS

PROMISES TO STAND ON

Promise: God is a master designer, and He designed your life. "Every day of my life was recorded in your book. Every moment was laid out before a single day had passed" (Psalm 139:16, NLT); "He has made everything beautiful in its time" (Ecclesiastes 3:11).

How do you feel as you read these words? Does it seem impossible that you will ever be able to call your experience "beautiful"? Do you long for relief from the burden of waiting for something you may never have? Do you wish you could just stop feeling any emotions at all?

Friend, I have met so many women who, like you, were deeply hurt by the sandstorm of infertility. Please don't give up hope in God's goodness. And please don't try to replace God's plan with your own. Consider Sarai, Abram's wife. God himself had promised to deliver a child through her, yet she grew impatient and resentful. This is understandable—after all, Sarai and Abram were both elderly. God's promise seemed less and less likely as years passed.

But Sarai's response was sinful and caused harm to others. When she told her husband to bear a child with their maidservant, Hagar, trouble brewed. This was a common practice in Old Testament times, but Sarai's seemingly simple solution backfired. Sarai's resentment only deepened; Hagar's pregnancy rankled the mistress of the house. Sarai's resulting mistreatment finally drove Hagar away. This was a no-win situation. Sarai certainly didn't speed up God's plan. Hagar's son didn't inherit Abram's riches and blessings. And Abram had two contentious women on his hands.

This is a good lesson to consider before we try to help God keep His promises! God doesn't need our guidance. In fact, we may only get in His way and make widening ripples of trouble. I guarantee it: Act like Sarai, try to rush God and force His hand, and you will end up frustrated and weakened. Act instead like a woman who believes in the One who made her and who planned for her a meaningful and rich life (Ephesians 2:10; 1 Timothy 6:17), and you will end up in the right place at the right time for the right plan.

What to do while you wait? Make your pain an offering to God.

Waiting patiently is an offering and a sacrifice. We may lift up our waiting to Him as a daily obligation, in a spirit of expectancy—like [a woman] who asks daily only for God's agenda. Waiting on God in *this* way is true faith—no agenda of one's own, no deadlines, no demands on what God must do. Simply an open heart and open hands to receive that which God shall choose, and in perfect confidence that what He chooses will be better than our best. God rewards that kind of faith.

"Never has ear heard or eye seen any other god taking the part of those who wait for him. Thou dost welcome him who rejoices to do what is right" [Isaiah 64:4-5, NEB].[1]

We will know the beauty of God's plan only as we let Him bring it about. Friend, let the storm rage—you rest.

Too many people miss the silver lining because they're expecting gold.
MAURICE SETTER

Promise: To use the old adage: The door God opens, no one can shut. "My word...will not return to Me empty, without accomplishing what I desire, and without succeeding in the matter for which I sent it" (Isaiah 55:11, NASB).

Expect that God will be glorified in your life. As you wait for His provision—of a child or of His graceful lifting of that desire—try taking these steps:

- Ask your husband to pray that you will conceive. "Issac prayed to the LORD on behalf of his wife, because she was barren. The LORD answered his prayer, and his wife Rebekah became pregnant" (Genesis 25:21).
- Read Hannah's story in 1 Samuel 1; then join with your husband and say the first few lines of Hannah's prayer every morning and night. Use this prayer to promise God that you

will raise a child in His light and instruction: "O LORD Almighty, if you will only look upon your servant's misery and remember me, and not forget your servant but give her a son, then I will give him to the LORD for all the days of his life" (1 Samuel 1:11).

- As a reminder to thank and praise God for the good gifts He brings you every morning and every night, buy a small picture frame, put this verse in it, and place it on your dresser or bedside table: "Every good and perfect gift is from above, coming down from the Father of the heavenly lights, who does not change like shifting shadows" (James 1:17).

- To build your faith, daily read one of the stories found throughout the Bible of other women and men who have struggled with having a baby. For example, refer to Rebekah's story in Genesis and Hannah's story in 1 Samuel.

- To keep your life clean and your spiritual armor shiny, seek forgiveness for anything in your life that might be displeasing to God. "Be strong in the Lord and in his mighty power" (Ephesians 6:10).

- Prepare for children by reading all you can about childbirth, motherhood, and raising children. "For wisdom will enter your heart, and knowledge will be pleasant to your soul. Discretion will protect you, and understanding will guard you" (Proverbs 2:10–11).

- Ask your friends and family to join in the prayer of faith for the conception or adoption of a child. "If two of you on earth agree about anything you ask for, it will be done for you by my Father in heaven" (Matthew 18:19).

- Join a Bible study and/or prayer group that will offer encouragement as well as prayer support. Ask for intercessory prayer concerning the desire of your heart. "For where two or three come together in my name, there am I with them" (Matthew 18:20).

- Search the Scriptures for God's promises and recite them. "He has given us his very great and precious promises, so that through them you may participate in the divine nature and escape the corruption in the world caused by evil desires" (2 Peter 1:4).
- Relinquish your desire to have a baby, and trust in the Lord with all your heart. "I trust in your unfailing love; my heart rejoices in your salvation. I will sing to the LORD, for he has been good to me" (Psalm 13:5–6).

Man can live about forty days without food,
about three days without water, about eight minutes without air…
but only for one second without hope.

HAL LINDSEY

CONCLUSION: HERE'S A TOWEL

Though some storms last for days, none are endless. Yours is fulfilling its course. And you never know what is on the other side.

Robin and Rick wanted children right away and began trying for them soon after their marriage. Months, and then years, flew by with no result. Finally a doctor's visit confirmed the worst: Pregnancy was a medical impossibility. The young couple was crushed.

Robin describes the anguish—do her words sound familiar? "My arms ached in emptiness. I stood facing the unattainable and looked at a life without children. I was powerless—no amount of work or schooling or money would bring a child to me. Together we mourned for the children we would never have.

"Whenever I saw a pregnant woman, I immediately seethed with envy. Did she know how blessed she was? Or did she take it all in stride, as a natural part of life?" Robin stopped attending baby showers given for family members and friends; she sent a gift instead.

Robin's story was not over. Deep within her, God's Spirit was stirring, sowing seeds of expectation. Robin gradually transitioned from weary resignation to unwavering hope. She found herself comforting Rick: "God has a plan for our family—it is just a different plan from our own."

The couple began submitting applications to adoption agencies. While other prospective parents waited years, Robin and Rick received a five-week-old baby within seven months. Of course, signing the final adoption papers was a momentous and life-changing experience. Hear Robin's radiant thoughts that day:

"Standing before the judge, I felt we were in the holiest of places. I looked down at my daughter's face, surrounded by a wavy thatch of black hair. Suddenly I thought, *This should be a ceremony with music and flowers in a garden. Friends and relatives should be in attendance to rejoice in this sacred moment. As in my wedding vows, a minister should unite us as a family. He should say, 'Do you take Kimberly to be your lawfully wedded daughter, to love and cherish, through sickness and health, for richer and poorer, as long as you shall live?' Then Rick and I should step forward and say, 'We do.'"*

As you wait to be united with your child, I hope you allow God to sow His contentment in your heart. I do not know what God will do in your life, but as we have seen, He is as loving and powerful now as He was when Elizabeth and Sarai craved motherhood. He can perform a miracle for you, too, whether it is the miracle of precious children or the miracle of perfect peace.

My friend, if you are feeling mud-splattered by the storm of infertility, dry off and put on a fresh slicker. His promise tells us that although the storm may not be over, it will pass.

The longest day must have its close—the gloomiest night will wear on to a morning. An eternal, inexorable lapse of moments is ever hurrying the day of the evil to an eternal night, and the night of the just to an eternal day.

HARRIET BEECHER STOWE

CHAPTER FOUR

LOOKING FOR PENNIES FROM HEAVEN

Security is not the absence of danger, but the presence of God, no matter what the danger.

ANONYMOUS

One of the most common and trying experiences is a lack of money. It is a desperate situation that tears at the soul from top to bottom. I'll bet you have been there—perhaps you have spent sleepless nights because your rent or mortgage was due, and you didn't have the money for it. Maybe you felt the pain of not being able to feed your family or buy needed medicine. Are bill collectors harassing you while you are forced to admit that the check not only isn't in the mail, it's nowhere to be found? Maybe you face unemployment, and despite the miles you've pounded on the sidewalks, no one wants to hire you. A money shortage is nothing short of a spiritual hurricane; it is one of the fiercest storms you may ever have to endure.

I've seen people pawn their treasures, visit the loan shark, and even sell off precious family heirlooms. Sometimes the burden of debt becomes so overwhelming, so impossible to resolve, that they must declare bankruptcy. They publicly admit their failure and begin to slowly rebuild their lives. And sometimes good, hardworking people, lacking any visible solution, give up altogether and take their own lives. Few storms have the power to drive us to such extreme measures.

Let's make something clear right away: Christians face money challenges just like everyone else. We make foolish investments and poor choices; we experience setbacks and failures. As far as the human experience goes, we're all in this together! But Christians have a resource that is uniquely comforting: We have God's promises. When the foundation is shaking, the stomach is growling, and the phone is ringing (or in the process of being disconnected), we have somewhere to go. It is right there in God's Word. God has given us all the answers!

GOD IS RELIABLE—RELY ON HIM!

Key Promise: "Do not worry, saying, 'What shall we eat?' or 'What shall we drink?' or 'What shall we wear?' For the pagans run after all these things, and your heavenly Father knows that you need them. But seek first his kingdom and his righteousness, and all these things will be given to you as well" (Matthew 6:31–33).

Friend, I have been there. The fear of financial ruin has been real to me on more than one occasion in my life. I've held my checkbook between shaking fingers as the balance turned out to be less than I expected. I've stared for days at bills that arrived in the mail, too afraid to open them. I've searched every pocket in my closet and every pocketbook I owned for loose change to pay an immediate bill. Yet God has been gracious enough to teach—and to keep teaching—me lessons about His unfailing goodness. On one very pivotal day He chose to speak to me through my daughter.

As a mom, I wanted passionately to ensure that Megan receive the same spiritual guidance with which I had been raised. It was these blessed assurances that had often kept me from being tossed about without direction in the midst of a financial storm.

One of the principles I chose to teach my daughter concerned tithing. I had been brought up to believe that it was important to give first to God, because it is in giving that we receive. Even if I were not blessed with worldly possessions to leave my daughter, I could bequeath her with a gift far greater: the faith that God would provide all her earthly needs.

How many times have you heard the statement, "If only I had more money, I could be happy"? My good friend, who handles investments for some of the wealthiest families in the United States, confided to me that she would also classify them as some of the *unhappiest* families in America. For this reason, it was important to teach my daughter that money doesn't buy happiness.

Every Sunday I watched Meg faithfully deposit her dollar bill in the offering plate. To my delight, Megan loved to do this. What she didn't know, though, was that on one particular Sunday her mother was not tithing—because I was frantically worried about my bank balance. The winds had begun to blow me off course; although I still clung to the Father, I had tied my purse strings in knots.

Meg smiled as she dropped her dollar in the plate. Then she leaned over and whispered, "Mom, does God fly down from heaven in a helicopter on Sunday afternoons to pick up His money?" I stifled a giggle as she repeated impatiently, "Mom, how does God get His money back up to heaven?"

"I'll tell you later," I said.

"I need to know now," she demanded. "Does God get the money or not?"

I tried to shush her. "In a way—I promise that I'll explain later."

"I thought I was giving that money to God," she said. "If He's not getting it, I want my money back."

Meg assumed that if God wasn't going to decide how to spend the money, then she didn't trust anyone other than herself to do it.

I assured her that our church would spend the money in the best way possible for God. My explanation seemed to satisfy her, but she commented later that day, "Mom, I understand the tithing part, but I think that God should be the one to decide how we spend our money."

I am so thankful that God gave me Meg, whom God often uses as an instrument of wisdom in my life. There I was, trying to teach her about tithing and trusting in God, and for the past few Sundays I had been unable to do either. I was hanging onto money out of the fear that God wouldn't meet my needs. Meg was right: God should decide how I spent my money.

This realization initiated a financial rebirth that took me straight to the Scriptures. I discovered God's promises concerning the thorny issue of supply and demand, and I realized that on this subject the Word is clear. We can trust God to provide all we need because He is God, and because He is loving. As the psalmist wrote:

> One thing God has spoken,
>   two things have I heard:
> that you, O God, are strong,
>   and that you, O Lord, are loving.
>   PSALM 62:11–12

God is strong. He is the King! When the blameless man Job challenged God's strength, God responded with, shall we say, a *convincing* description of His capabilities. Like Job, wouldn't you have been left speechless after God spoke these words to you?

> Who set its measurements, since you know?
>   Or who stretched the line on it?
> On what were its bases sunk?

Or who laid its cornerstone,
When the morning stars sang together,
  And all the sons of God shouted for joy?
Or who enclosed the sea with doors,
  When, bursting forth, it went out from the womb;
When I made a cloud its garment,
  And thick darkness its swaddling band,
And I placed boundaries on it,
  And I set a bolt and doors.
And I said, "Thus far you shall come, but no farther;
  And here you shall your proud waves stop"?

JOB 38:5–11, NASB

As Psalm 62 says, not only is our King strong, but He is also lov-ing. Not only is He the One who stretched land over sea and dotted the sky with stars, but He is also a personal God who is vitally inter-ested in our ups and downs, our delights and our dilemmas. Peter wrote, "Let him have all your worries and cares, for he is always thinking about you and watching everything that concerns you" (1 Peter 5:7, TLB). "He will never let me stumble, slip or fall. For he is always watching, never sleeping" (Psalm 121:3–4, TLB).

My heavenly Father had promised to help me through this storm. I had His assurance that He would strengthen me to face whatever came. I realized that, like Peter trying to walk on the water, I would not sink if I kept my eyes on Jesus instead of the threaten-ing sea of bills!

Friend, these truths about God, these aspects of His unchang-ing character, form the foundation of trust we can rest upon when financial gusts blow. God says that as we seek pure faith in Him (His righteousness), He will deal with the earthly needs that overshadow us. The promises that God makes *stand true*—through every storm. Let me share my experience of that certainty.

Money is always dull, except when you haven't got any,
and then it's terrifying.

SHEILA BISHOP

FLEAS AND FLAT TIRES

Years ago I read the story of Corrie and Betsie ten Boom, sisters who were imprisoned in a concentration camp as punishment for hiding Jews from the Nazis. You may have read it also. One day they awoke to find their cell block infested with thousands of fleas. The fleas were biting, stinging, and making the prisoners even more miserable.

The sisters had an inspiration. They remembered the way that Paul and Silas responded to their imprisonment—with singing (Acts 16:25–34). Corrie and Betsie began praising God for the fleas. Just think what the other women in their building must have thought. I can imagine them whispering, "Those ten Boom sisters have finally gone off the deep end! Do you hear them praising and thanking God for these fleas?"

How they must have changed their tune when they saw that the sisters' praise released a great blessing. Because the German officers didn't want to be bitten by the fleas, they avoided this particular cell block. The prisoners realized that those menacing fleas saved many of them from more cruel treatment—or even death!

This lesson returned to me one dark day when I was facing my own vermin. Peggy Dickinson Watkins, another single parent with a daughter, and I had traded the luxury of a regular paycheck for the flexibility of owning our own business. We had established a unique management consulting business that provided an interviewing service for clients. This allowed us to attend our daughters' school plays, to carpool, and to become more involved in the girls' hobbies and interests. With this new freedom came the responsibility of raising my daughter, meeting financial obligations, and running a business and a home. Each day proved to be a challenging but fulfilling experience.

On this particular day, the coming month loomed before us, empty and ominous, with no assignments in sight. We tried to be optimistic—that very morning we were scheduled to meet with the human resources director at a large company that had numerous job openings. We hoped that by the time the next month rolled around, our bank account would have been replenished with the hiring fees from this company.

Things looked good—at first. "Your service sounds great," the man behind the desk said enthusiastically.

I threw Peggy a broad smile.

"However," he continued, "our company is not authorized to pay outside fees for hiring."

Peggy and I stopped smiling. Empty-handed, we drove back to the office in silence, lost in our private worries. I contemplated the things that had transpired in my life since I had met Peggy. God had been so faithful, so generous in His provision, that I knew he wouldn't desert me now.

Deep in thought, I became so distracted that I hit the curb and burst the tire on my car. This expense was not in my budget. I was instantly heartsick, especially since I could have avoided this accident. Fortunately, a service station was right across the street.

The mechanic delivered the dismal news that my tire could not be repaired and must be replaced. How would I make ends meet? All the confidence that had been building just minutes before dissolved.

I knew that I could either burst into tears or trust God. Suddenly, I remembered Corrie ten Boom. If this great lady and her sister could praise God in the midst of those fleas, I could praise God for my flat tire. Anyway, I figured it beat crying.

I said aloud, "Father, I am trusting You in this circumstance. You can bring good out of my busted tire."

Peggy looked at me as though I had lost my mind. "Let me get this straight. You're thanking God for your flat tire?"

I nodded. She shook her head.

The service station manager told us that it would be at least an hour before the car was ready. "Well, we can't just sit around here," I told Peggy. "There's an office next door. Since we have all our presentation books and brochures, why don't we knock on some doors?" Peggy had trained me, and she was always pleased when I suggested that we make cold calls. We walked over to the building.

The two of us went from floor to floor, dropping off brochures and asking to meet human resource directors. None were available, but we gathered several names and set later appointments. At the third floor we were surprised to find every office door locked. Curious, we hurried to the next floor to inquire about the phantom company below.

"They outgrew that space," a woman informed us. "They're one of the fastest growing companies in America."

"Do you know where they moved?" I asked.

"They've taken over the entire building next door."

It was music to our ears! Peggy suggested, "Let's go!"

We hurried to the adjacent building and asked for information about the company at the front desk. The director of marketing came out of his office and offered to give us a tour of the facility. As we waited in the lobby for the director to gather some company brochures, the president suddenly appeared. I knew this was a divine appointment! I boldly stood up and asked, "Aren't you Mr. Jones?"

"Why, yes!" he replied, obviously pleased to be recognized. "How did you know?"

"I've seen your picture everywhere." It wasn't a lie; I had seen his picture on almost every wall in the offices of the company!

"And who might you be?" he inquired with interest.

I quickly explained who we were and what we did.

"Sounds intriguing," he replied. "We're doing a lot of hiring. If you will stick around until I get back from lunch, I'd like to hear what you have to say."

He checked with his secretary and made an appointment with us right there on the spot. We walked away equipped not only with valuable new information concerning the company, but also with an appointment that very afternoon with its president and CEO!

The rest is history. Peggy and I landed the account, and it proved so lucrative that we were able to pay all of our expenses, as well as to expand our business over the next few years. Had I not hit the curb that day when all hope seemed lost, we might never have discovered that company or acquired its account when we needed it the most! God met our needs and more.

When people later asked me how we obtained an account that many others in Atlanta were pursuing, I smiled and said, "Would you believe that it came about through thanking the Lord for a flat tire?"

There have been other faith-inspiring incidents in my life, but none quite so profound as my flat tire. It taught me the lasting lesson that faith pleases our heavenly Father. We honor Him with our trust. When circumstances appear insurmountable and you are deflated, *thank* God, for He is strong and loving, full of wonders just waiting to unfold. "Cast your cares on the LORD and he will sustain you; he will never let the righteous fall" (Psalm 55:22).

God and His promises are dependable! Rely on Him. Let me share some other stories about His unfailing provision.

Be like the bird that, passing on her flight awhile on boughs too slight,
feels them give way beneath her, and yet sings,
knowing that she hath wings.

VICTOR HUGO

THE KEY—TRUST; THE TEST—TITHE

My friend's daughter, Hannah, had more than her share of troubles. After a bitter legal battle, she lost custody of her two little boys and was ordered to make child-support payments each month. In addition, in order to be close to the children, she had to leave her family and friends and move to a small town where she knew no one. There was little employment opportunity in the town, and Hannah ended up working as a waitress in a restaurant.

Hers was a lonely life; the hours were long and the work stressful and exhausting. Between rent, child-support payments, and other expenses, Hannah could barely make ends meet. Her family was unable to help her monetarily, but her mother was a godly woman who believed firmly in honoring God through financial difficulty. "You must tithe, Hannah," she told her daughter gently.

Maybe you have felt as Hannah did when she heard her mother: *Are you kidding? I can't pay all the bills as it is! Wouldn't God want me to be responsible and use the income for expenses?* Hannah didn't have a dime to spare, so she chose to ignore her mother's advice. Her circumstances grew worse. Her car needed new tires, her refrigerator stopped running, and she had no dental coverage.

After a particularly difficult day, Hannah called home in tears. Once again her mother encouraged her to tithe. Hannah confessed that she didn't believe tithing would help, but decided, nonetheless, to follow her mother's advice. Though she struggled, each week she tithed.

A few weeks later Hannah waited on an elderly gentlemen in the restaurant. When he left, she was stunned to discover that he had left $1200 on the table. This couldn't be her tip! He must have left the money accidentally.

Hannah ran out of the restaurant and tried to catch the man, but he was nowhere in sight. She walked back in and gave her manager the money.

"That's some tip," the manager commented.

"It must be a mistake," Hannah said, sighing. "The poor man will probably be worried sick when he discovers his money is missing."

"I'll tell you what, Hannah," her boss said. "I'll keep the money for a month. If he doesn't come in to claim it, I'm going to assume that this was your tip."

The man never returned, and Hannah got her big tip! Her response to the windfall blessing? "I tithed on it," Hannah says. "And I've been tithing ever since."

It's a beautiful lesson. Hannah trusted God with her little, and God in turn trusted her with much. The story has an even happier ending. Hannah continued to work hard and struggle for more than ten years, but she continued to tithe and God continued to provide. Last year the Lord blessed her with a husband of great wealth, and Hannah has influenced this godly man to do important and helpful things with his money. Hannah passed God's test in the midst of the storm.

Have you, too, been in a furnace? Has fear swallowed your courage and locked your pocketbook? The point I'm trying to make is not so much a lesson on tithing as it is an attempt to encourage you to trust God in whatever circumstance you find yourself. When you honor God, He will honor you.

Wealth consists not in having great possessions but in having few wants.

ESTHER DE WAAL

A HAPPY CYCLE

My friend Betty has one of the most generous hearts I know. For many years, she was not only the breadwinner for her family but also the sole provider for her children and for her invalid mother. Betty always gives what she has; when she is unable to give money, she gives of herself.

During the sixties and early seventies, Betty and her husband ran a children's theater in Atlanta. Both of them were committed to the arts and took their workshop throughout the housing projects in the city, sharing drama with underprivileged children.

One day Betty received a call from a woman asking if her children could join the workshop as students. "Of course," she replied without hesitation. This was a more courageous decision than it may sound. You see, the call came from Mrs. Coretta Scott King, and the year was 1966. Mrs. King explained that many of the acting schools in Atlanta refused to admit black students. Betty was outraged over this. She assured Mrs. King that the workshop would welcome her children into the program. That day Betty gave Mrs. King her unprejudiced heart.

This was the first integrated theater in Atlanta, and many people were openly critical of Betty and her husband for allowing African-American students to perform on stage along with white students. Even when the school's enrollment began to decline, Betty stood firmly on her principles and put her beliefs before her pocketbook. She refused to give into the racial pressures of the era.

Anyone who has worked in the theater knows that money is scarce, and this acting school was no exception; they had their share of financial struggles, but trusted God for the outcome. When Betty delivered their third child, a little girl whom they named Julie, the family struggled to pay the hospital bill. Betty treated the bill as she did any other problem—she prayed.

No one could have predicted how God would answer. When Coretta Scott King heard about Betty's plight, she wrote a check to the hospital. Mrs. King was not a wealthy woman; she was merely giving back to a woman who had given to her.

And the cycle continues. When Mrs. King wrote that check, she had no idea that baby girl would grow up to be Julia Roberts, one of the most famous and talented actresses of all time. But God knew! More than twenty years later the actress has in turn con-

tributed to Coretta Scott King's charitable foundation, the Martin
Luther King Jr. Center for Social Change.

Three women helped to form this story, but God empowers it.
Trust in Him creates generosity, which regenerates itself. The writer
of Ecclesiastes encourages, "Cast your bread upon the waters, for
after many days you will find it again" (Ecclesiastes 11:1).

Hope is putting faith to work when doubting would be easier.

ANONYMOUS

PROMISES TO STAND ON

Promise: Your needs are God's problem. "Consider the ravens: They do
not sow or reap, they have no storeroom or barn; yet God feeds them.
And how much more valuable you are than birds!... But seek his kingdom, and these things will be given you as well" (Luke 12:24, 31).

Friend, the answer is simple: God is our provider. Life may look
dark—too dark even for His miraculous surprises—but what we see
means little. What we *know* is everything. The prophet Jeremiah
wisely wrote:

Blessed is the man who trusts in the LORD,
  whose confidence is in him.
He will be like a tree planted by the water
  that sends out its roots by the stream.
It does not fear when heat comes;
  its leaves are always green.
It has no worries in a year of drought
  and never fails to bear fruit.

JEREMIAH 17:7–8

What an inspiring picture! We can stand like a tree with roots deep
in well-watered ground, healthy, assured, and laden with good fruit

even in dry seasons. This is possible as we learn to commit every detail of our lives, especially the confusing and frightening circumstances, to the King. As we practice faith, His love makes us confident. I especially like the way the recent Bible translation *The Message* puts Jesus' words:

> "Walk into the fields and look at the wildflowers. They don't fuss with their appearance—but have you ever seen color and design quite like it? The ten best-dressed men and women in the country look shabby alongside them. If God gives such attention to the wildflowers, most of them never even seen, don't you think he'll attend to you, take pride in you, do his best for you?
>
> "What I'm trying to do here is get you to relax, not be so preoccupied with *getting* so that you can respond to God's *giving*. People who don't know God and the way he works fuss over these things, but you know both God and how he works. Steep yourself in God-reality, God-initiative, God-provisions. You'll find all your everyday human concerns will be met." (Luke 12:27–31, *The Message*)

As we have seen throughout this chapter, God is faithful and true through changing circumstances. Lean on Him.

> *To eat bread without hope is still to slowly starve to death.*
> PEARL S. BUCK

Promise: God rewards your giving. "You must each make up your own mind as to how much you should give. Don't give reluctantly or in response to pressure. For God loves the person who gives cheerfully. And God will generously provide all you need. Then you will always have everything you need and plenty left over to share with others" (2 Corinthians 9:7–8, NLT).

Give trustingly; do not focus on what you don't have. Keep your
eyes on Him and not on your bank balance.

Give expectantly; know that God will provide for all your needs
according to His riches in glory.

Give joyfully; realize that God blesses giving—and trust.

Give gratefully; acknowledge all the blessings that God has
given to you.

Give lavishly; know that you cannot outgive God!

Our greatest good, and what we least can spare, is hope.

JOHN ARMSTRONG

Promise: The Lord is our safe haven. "Taste and see that the LORD
is good; blessed is the man who takes refuge in him. Fear the LORD,
you his saints, for those who fear him lack nothing" (Psalm 34:8–9).

How do we find out how good the Lord is? When He calls us
to do the difficult—give up worry; trust Him to guide us through a
financial ordeal; let Him provide what we cannot—we do it. We let
adversity drive us toward Him, not away from Him. We watch and
we witness: His promises are true! "The name of the LORD is a strong
tower; the righteous run to it and are safe" (Proverbs 18:10).

When God seems long in answering, we wait, and we keep hoping. We believe that diligence is something God honors. Jesus
taught, "Ask and it will be given to you; seek and you will find;
knock and the door will be opened to you. For everyone who asks
receives; he who seeks finds; and to him who knocks, the door will
be opened" (Matthew 7:7–8).

When our resources are lean, we respond with abiding faith. We
give to others—either of our finances or of our time and energy:
"Give, and it will be given to you. A good measure, pressed down,
shaken together and running over, will be poured into your lap. For
with the measure you use, it will be measured to you" (Luke 6:38).

Hope is faith holding out its hand in the dark.

GEORGE ILES

CONCLUSION: YOU CAN HIDE IN HIS HAND

Yes, the raindrops sting as they pelt the skin. The water pools on your shoulders and sends icy trickles cascading down your back. The wind whips your hair into your eyes. A financial storm is uncomfortable, often nearly unbearable.

But an amazing result is within reach. Consider the story my friend told me about her grandfather. Decades ago, this young man risked every dime he had to go to Texas to find oil. After several years his pockets—and his potential oil wells—were empty. He had enough money left to either dig one more time or to purchase a small ranch on the outskirts of town.

He and his wife prayed. She soon felt God impress a Scripture on her heart: "He who works his land will have abundant food, but he who chases fantasies lacks judgment" (Proverbs 12:11). She encouraged her husband to buy the ranch.

The man hesitated. On the one hand, he had a passionate dream of oil riches. But on the other hand, he had the Word's seemingly clear direction. He could lean on his ambition and hope for luck, or he could lean on the Lord and hope for redemption.

He bought the ranch. Initially, this effort also failed. The ranch generated little money. Food was scarce. Then came the last straw: The well ran dry. Repeated digging yielded only dust. Beginning to despair, the man lamented, "If only we'd gone for the black gold."

"No," his wife assured him. "We're in the Lord's hand. Try again."

In a final attempt to enable his family to remain, the rancher dug another well. Once again he didn't find water, but this time his well wasn't dry. The rancher hit—you guessed it—*oil!* Lots of it. The fortune has lasted several generations and continues to support the Lord's work in many arenas.

Friend, don't stand in the rain. Hang onto His umbrella with one hand and keep digging those wells with the other. Hide beneath His shelter until the storm blows over. You can rest in His safe provision.

The fire that seems so cruel is the light that shows your strength.

ELLA WHEELER-WILCOX

CHAPTER FIVE

CAUGHT UP
IN A WHIRLWIND

*The real stuff of life was experience, in which sorrow and fear
and disaster had as important a part to play as beauty and joy.*
SHEILA KAYE-SMITH

*I*t's the shrill ring of the phone in the middle of the night.
It's the shake of the house on its foundation as forceful
winds assault, an eerie darkness suddenly falling. It's the
heartbeat you feel in your throat as a hooded figure points a gun at
you and makes demands.

Whether it's a natural calamity such as an earthquake or a flood,
a physical catastrophe that steals a loved one's life, or the terrifying
reality of being robbed or attacked, the disaster is another of those
storms that seems to touch each one of us. Because of its nature—it
is always unexpected—this storm is uniquely crippling. How can
anyone ever be prepared for a terrible diagnosis, a home invasion,
or a tornado that appears on a cloudless spring day? When these
things happen, each of us tastes terror in a new and life-changing
way. The result of disaster is traumatic and never short-lived. Is it
any wonder our faith often shatters in the aftermath? Who among
us hasn't wondered, *Where was God when this happened? What did I
do to deserve this? How will I live without my loved one? Will life ever be
normal again?*

While we cannot physically anticipate these experiences, we can be spiritually prepared. We can build a faith that stands strong in gales. For those who are enduring such calamities today, use the same lesson to bolster your faith, which this storm has attacked mercilessly. You need not collapse—the will and the strength of your Father can put you back on your feet. Friend, come and learn how to stand.

GOD IS YOUR SAFE CENTER

Key Promise: "God is a safe place to hide, ready to help when we need him. We stand fearless at the cliff-edge of doom, courageous in seastorm and earthquake, before the rush and roar of oceans, the tremors that shift mountains" (Psalm 46:1–3, *The Message*).

My heart aches when I read of the lives lost in major catastrophes. We've all heard the gut-wrenching story of the baby being ripped from his mother's arms in a tornado, or the destruction of a church during Sunday service that killed several of its members. I groan inwardly when I hear about a young person killed in a drive-by shooting or a father perishing in a fire. The agony felt by a woman who has suffered at the hands of a rapist or an abuser is almost too horrible to comprehend. In response I cry out to my heavenly Father, who for some reason chose not to intervene in these tragedies.

When such events occur, some refer to them as "acts of God." Others fight the idea that God would allow such pain in the human race. Before we learn how to stand in the storm of a calamity, we need to consider this question: Does God let awful things happen to His people?

Scripture is clear on this topic. Throughout the Bible, God acknowledges His hand in specific disasters: "I form the light and create darkness, I bring prosperity and create disaster; I, the LORD, do all these things" (Isaiah 45:7). Take, for instance, the flood that destroyed all of mankind but spared Noah and his family. The Lord announced that the flood was His doing: "I am going to bring flood-waters on the earth to destroy all life under the heavens, every creature that has the breath of life in it. Everything on earth will perish" (Genesis 6:17).

Though in Noah's case the Lord spared the righteous, he does not always do this. Jesus said, "Your Father in heaven...causes his sun to rise on the evil and the good, and sends rain on the righteous and the unrighteous" (Matthew 5:45). We see evidence of this truth just by looking around. We can all point to folks who love God yet are dealt some of life's harshest blows. Look at Job—he was a righteous man whom God allowed to suffer at Satan's hand. Despite what we wish to be true, the fact remains that God is in control of every event that befalls mankind, either by causing or by allowing each to occur.

This truth can be either terrifying or reassuring. Aren't you glad to know that God filters every experience that happens to us—that nothing "slips by" without His permission? That may offer little comfort in the midst of your trial, but Scripture is very clear on this point: He is a loving God. Don't your blessings outnumber your pains? Don't you find, even in the darkest of storms, a beam of His light shining through and bringing you comfort? Haven't you felt His care through the Christlike actions of a good friend? Remember, the ultimate expression of God's love was to send His Son for our redemption. Zechariah, father of John the Baptist, praised "the tender mercy of our God, by which the rising sun will come to us from heaven to shine on those living in darkness and in the shadow of death, to guide our feet into the path of peace" (Luke 1:78–79).

This is how we make sense of two truths: Because God is all-powerful, we know that He allows every circumstance we encounter in life; because God is all-loving, we know that He never leaves us to face these circumstances alone. Our key promise reminds us that

He is "an ever-present help *in* trouble" (Psalm 46:1, emphasis mine). If He were not all-powerful, He would not be worthy of our worship; if He were not loving, He would not be worthy of our devotion.

I know that these are enormous theological issues, which lie beyond the scope of this book. Suffice it to say that as believers, we have evidence proving that God is both strong and loving. Friend, let's find the help God offers us. It comes not by hoping that we will never experience pain, but by believing that we will never have to endure it alone. We can trust Him to help us hold our own in the storm. I have proof—read on!

> *The light of God surrounds me,*
> *The love of God enfolds me,*
> *The power of God protects me,*
> *The Presence of God watches over me,*
> *Wherever I am, God is.*
>
> PRAYER CARD

UP CLOSE AND PERSONAL: THE BARREL OF A GUN

Calamity has literally struck close to home in my own life. My husband endured one of the most frightening situations that anyone can experience. I'll let him tell the story.

Susan and Meg had just left when the doorbell rang. Checking the peephole, I saw four young men. Because we lived near the high school, kids often dropped by our home on their way to the park that overlooks the ocean at the end of our street. Assuming they were friends of my teenage stepdaughter, I opened the door.

"Meg's not at home; may I help you?" I said. When they hesitated, I instinctively knew that I was in trouble. The four of them, all wearing black hooded parkas, pushed their way inside. One of them thrust a gun into my stomach, and another shoved me into our living room.

You may wonder what thoughts ran through my mind. I am fortunate; because my father was a pastor for fifty-three years, I have been spoon-fed the Word since I was a small child. The words of a psalm I had learned years earlier kept me from panicking:

> The LORD is my light and my salvation—
>   whom shall I fear?
> The LORD is the stronghold of my life—
>   of whom shall I be afraid?
> When evil men advance against me
>   to devour my flesh,
> when my enemies and my foes attack me,
>   they will stumble and fall.
> Though an army besiege me,
>   my heart will not fear;
> though war break out against me,
>   even then will I be confident.
>
> PSALM 27:1–3

"Don't look at me!" one of the young men screamed, punctuating the order with profanity.

Three of the men surrounded me, moving the gun to the back of my neck. One of them told me to keep my eyes closed and my head down. I obeyed. All three shouted obscenities as they gagged me, then put a pillowcase over my head and tied it around my neck.

I began to gasp for air. Pushing me down on the floor, they bound my legs and hands. Still the Lord kept me in perfect peace as I repeated the Scriptures in my mind: "Have no fear of sudden disaster or of the ruin that overtakes the wicked, for the LORD will be your confidence and will keep your foot from being snared" (Proverbs 3:25–26).

Though I couldn't see and was struggling to breathe, I felt calmness surround me. One of the men pressed the cold metal of the gun barrel against my head through the pillowcase. Certain that I was about to die, I quickly whispered Jesus' final prayer: "Into your hands I commit my spirit." I heard the man cock the gun; he screamed obscenities at me as he pulled the trigger. Miraculously, the gun did not fire. This angered the young men, and they began kicking me in the back and in the head. I winced in pain but silently quoted, "I shall not die, but live, and declare the works of the LORD" (Psalm 118:17, KJV).

The men then turned their attention to ransacking the house. I could hear them moving things around, picking some up, throwing others. I silently concentrated on the words from Psalm 118:17. A heavy foot pressed into my back, and one of the men ordered, "Don't move and don't say a word." With my head covered by the pillowcase and my mouth gagged, I began to feel lightheaded. I prayed that my wife and daughter would not return. I prayed that God would protect them. I came to as I heard the pounding of heavy shoes gathering around me again. They administered more kicks to my back.

One of the men spoke up. "We're leaving. Don't move until we've been gone for a couple of hours. We'll be back to check on you." I heard the door slam and silently thanked God that I was alive. I reached up to loosen the pillowcase; just as I got it off of my head, the door flew open again, and one of the young men raged, "Put that back over your head!" I quickly obeyed. He charged at me and held the gun to my head. He cocked it, and when he pulled the trigger, it misfired a second time. He kicked me before he departed, spewing a string of obscenities. I lay there for what seemed like an eternity, afraid to move.

After a while I pulled the pillowcase from my head and looked around. I was alone. Although badly bruised, I managed to get to my feet. I walked to the phone and dialed 9-1-1, praising God that He had spared my life.

Susan: When I returned, I was horrified to find our home surrounded by police cars with flashing lights. The house looked as though a tornado had swept through the center of it. The attackers had taken almost everything of value, but I was so happy to find Ken alive and not seriously hurt that the loss meant nothing.

Slowly we recovered. Ken was a changed man after the burglary. His faith was as strong as ever, but he realized how close to death he'd come and often insisted, "I've got to make the rest of my life count. God spared me for a purpose."

Ken's story is a good example of the horrors Christians may be called to face. The key to his mental clarity in the midst of the attack was the spiritual preparation from his childhood. Quoting Scriptures brought God's presence close when Ken felt most alone—face-to-face with angry young men, threatened with a firearm, and no one to call on but God Himself. The Father was present in Ken's pain. And Ken knew, in spite of the threats he faced, that he was neither forgotten nor lost from God's sight, but instead held lovingly: "What is the price of five sparrows? A couple of pennies? Not much more than that. Yet God does not forget a single one of them. And he knows the number of hairs on your head! Never fear, you are far more valuable to him than a whole flock of sparrows" (Luke 12:6–7, TLB). The Lord was Ken's confidence.

It's a good thing to have all the props
pulled out from under us occasionally.
It gives us some sense of what is rock under our feet, and what is sand.
MADELEINE L'ENGLE

CAN EVIL PENETRATE GOD'S PROTECTION?

What do we do when God allows evil to pervade, even after we have prayed for protection? My friend Leigh Jansen, a wonderful Christian girl, had to face this very question. She shared her tragic storm story with me.

In college, I joined a fundamentalist church organization and met a young man who appeared sincere in his faith. Since I had grown up a Christian, faith in God was a prerequisite for my future husband. When Scott and I began to date, we attended Bible studies and prayed together. I thought we were meant for each other, and after several months we began to consider marriage.

I was completely unprepared for what happened one warm spring night. Scott had invited me over to watch television. When I arrived, I found that his roommate was out on a date, which left us alone in the apartment. As we cuddled on the couch, watching our favorite show, we shared a few kisses. Suddenly Scott began grabbing at me. I told him "No!" several times and tried to push him away.

It's as though he turned into someone I didn't even know. He shoved me down onto the couch and proceeded to rape me as I sobbed and pleaded with him to stop. The last thing I remember seeing was the picture of a smiling Jesus hanging over the couch. My eyes locked onto the eyes of my Savior. *Help me, please.*

"In God have I put my trust: I will not be afraid what man can do unto me" (Psalm 56:11, KJV). The verse that I had loved as a child filled my mind, yet the reality remained that this man was doing something to me I both feared and hated, and that I was powerless to stop him. I didn't understand. If God was omnipotent, how could He allow this to happen to me? Why didn't He protect me?

Later, I limped into the bathroom and locked the door. I was bleeding and shaking. Scott resumed watching television as though nothing had happened. I spent an hour locked in the tiny bathroom, trying to get my thoughts together. *Where did I go wrong? What did I do to incite this?* In a single evening, I had become damaged goods. I finally walked back into the living room, a false smile pasted on my face; I was too scared and embarrassed to discuss the unpleasantness of what had just happened.

I sat numbly across the room from Scott, pretending that I was interested in the television show. Soon Scott was ready to take me home. I pulled away when he tried to kiss me good night at my dormitory front door. I was ashamed, angry, and very confused. I wanted to tell my roommate what had happened, but I was afraid that she would think less of me.

I had always wanted to be a role model, a good example. Now I felt like a pile of trash. Perhaps I could still pretend that I was the same Christian girl who had stepped out hours earlier to spend an innocent evening with her boyfriend.

My parents had raised me to believe that the first time to experience sex was on the wedding night, but I had been taken against my will. The phrase *date rape* had not yet been coined, but it still happened. Until that night, I had saved myself for my husband—and it had been taken from me against my will. What should have been a beautiful gift was now nonrefundable.

Though I had lost all respect for Scott, I felt duty-bound to marry him. After several tormented months, something inside me snapped. I broke up with Scott. I also left my faith. I felt that God had let me down, so it was natural that I should let Him down, too. I went my own way in life.

It took many years for me to realize that what had happened was rape and that it was not my fault. Perhaps if I had counseled with my pastor I could have better handled the trauma and ultimately avoided much of the pain. But the truth of the matter was that I was afraid. I thought that my pastor would confirm my deepest fear: that I got what I deserved for putting myself into a questionable situation. I was already caving beneath the burden of guilt.

I did everything I knew to escape the situation. I closed myself off from family, friends, and God. The years following the incident were difficult. I had no victory in my life. A maverick lifestyle took over.

After graduating from college, I landed a teaching job. Two of the teachers with whom I worked were Christians, and they witnessed to me in many ways, each one greatly irritating. Yet they were patient and kind, virtues I had not seen in a long time. I did not realize it then, but God was calling me back to Himself, away from the hatred and the confusion. He saw my hurt and my heartbreak, loving me even though I felt unloved and unworthy of love.

One night I knelt beside my couch and prayed, remembering how safe and warm I had felt as a child of God. A voice inside me said that I could feel that way again. I poured out all of my hurt and disillusionment. I was an angry, bruised little girl that night as I wept and pounded the floor with my fists. How could someone I loved and trusted do this to me? Suddenly I was sorry for all the foolish decisions I had made, ready to seek forgiveness. I knew that in order to begin rebuilding my life, I had to forgive Scott. It was difficult, a decision I had to make in my mind before I could feel it in my heart.

I opened my clenched fists and raised them to heaven, asking God to take the anger and the hurt. I finally felt free to become a whole person. It was a though I had come home. Laughter and joy returned to my life. What had happened became a single incident in a lifetime of experiences. It no longer consumed me.

I have learned that being a Christian doesn't mean life will be easy. It *does* mean that I have help to overcome any problem life may bring my way. I give each problem to Jesus, who loved me and gave His life for me. Yes, I saw the picture of Jesus looking down at me on that fateful night. He was watching over me even then. He brought me safely back home to Him.

Did forgiveness erase the nightmares? Have I given up asking God why these things had to happen to me? No. I realize today that the verse does ring with truth: Faith in God means that nothing man can do has the power to harm me eternally, that God always has the last word. And that word is *love*.

It's a truth I am teaching my own daughter and son.

Leigh took the worst life threw at her and responded with the best God had to give: forgiveness. Healing. Restoration.

Not every rape victim will recover in the same way that Leigh did, but every storm victim can be a survivor. She can experience God's redemption in the midst of unbearable, inexplicable pain. With time and faith, she can know the truth of God's Word: "We know how much God loves us because we have felt his love and because we believe him when he tells us that he loves us dearly…. Our love for him comes as a result of his loving us first" (1 John 4:16, 19, TLB).

Do you need some cover from a storm today? Quick, come under God's umbrella. Find Him to be your safe center in life's whirlwind.

I long to put the experience of fifty years at once into your young lives,
to give you at once the key to that treasure chamber every gem
of which has cost me tears and struggles and prayers,
but you must work for these inward treasures yourselves.
HARRIET BEECHER STOWE

THE CALIFORNIA EXPERIENCE—COMPLETE WITH EARTHQUAKE

In January 1994 we had just returned to Los Angeles from filming another season of the CBS series *Christy* in Tennessee. After a restless night, I finally drifted to sleep, only to be rudely awakened by the mournful howling of dogs. I heard a deep, inexplicable creaking and moaning; then everything began to shake violently.

It is the end of the world, I thought. Then the house tipped from right to left and literally bounced off its foundation. Shocked and scared, I reached across the king-sized bed for my husband—but he wasn't there. I began screaming his name. "Ken, Ken! Where are you?"

I heard things crashing all through the house, glass breaking and wood splintering and collapsing. *Maybe this isn't the end of the world—maybe this is an earthquake!*

I hung onto the sheets for dear life. A picture fell from the wall, narrowly missing me, and the lamp on my bedside table hit me in the head. The terror of feeling absolutely no control over my surroundings was indescribable. I had read about earthquakes, had seen them on television and in the movies, and had heard the horror stories. Still, nothing can prepare a person for the real thing. My southern friends had teased me about earthquakes when I moved to California, and their predictions appeared true: It felt as though California really were falling into the ocean.

Dear God, I prayed, *please be with me. Hold me in your arms.* I screamed again for Ken. "Where are you?"

Still no answer. Maybe he'd been thrown from our house. I quickly breathed a prayer for his safety. I wondered, *Has he been raptured and left me behind?* Wild with terror, I began praying for myself.

I thought of my parents. They were probably awake by now on the East Coast. Little did they know that their daughter was about to die in an earthquake. I sadly realized that I would probably never see them again. Terror began to engulf me.

Calm down, I told myself. I didn't know which was trembling more—the earth or me. And then I remembered the Scripture, "God is our refuge and strength, an ever-present help in trouble. Therefore we will not fear, though the earth give way and the mountains fall into the heart of the sea, though its waters roar and foam and the mountains quake with their surging" (Psalm 46:1–3).

When I had memorized this promise as a child, I had no idea what lay ahead—how much I would need every word of God's promise. I felt His peace begin to enfold me. The earth was still shaking, but I was calm. I felt the Savior's presence.

Suddenly, Ken came around the corner. Thirty-six seconds had passed and the earth stood still at last.

Ken was safe and so was I. He immediately turned on the radio and television for coverage of the quake; we watched in horror at the reports of damage and death. We felt so blessed to be safe and in each other's arms as we listened to the stories of pain and grief.

We walked through our house, surveying the wreckage. Almost everything had been damaged. Looking around at the shattered remains, we were in a state of shock. Ken began to put the furniture upright, and I knelt to pick up the pieces of our broken possessions. Ordinarily I would have been heartbroken to lose so many treasures, but at the moment all that mattered was that we were alive—that God had spared us in the earthquake.

Every few minutes a violent aftershock would rock us, a reminder of the terror we had just endured. These continued for over a year and served to maintain a certain tension in the air. I didn't feel normal again for months.

Ken and I found that life becomes precious when you live through catastrophe. Life lessons, like earthquakes, teach us to depend upon our heavenly Father. God does hold our future in His hand, and we were grateful for His comfort and love, as well as for strength and courage in the days that followed the storm.

We shall steer safely through every storm, so long as our heart is right,
our intention fervent, our courage steadfast, and
our trust fixed on God. If at times we are somewhat stunned
by the tempest, never fear. Let us take breath, and go on afresh.

FRANCIS DE SALES

PROMISES TO STAND ON

Promise: God has equipped you to handle storms. "God has not given us a spirit of fear and timidity, but of power, love, and self-discipline" (2 Timothy 1:7, NLT).

No one knows when disaster will strike. Instead of worrying about this, we should instead focus on our preparedness. God has instilled in us a source of help: His Holy Spirit. I experienced the Spirit's presence during the earthquake, when a supernatural calm settled me down—even though my house was shaking, my husband was missing, and my heart was pounding! The Holy Spirit brings power, love, and self-discipline—just the antidote for our natural inclination to feel helplessness, hate, and panic. Jesus called the Spirit "the Counselor," whom God would send to believers to teach us and remind us of Jesus' words (John 14:26). Paul taught that "the Spirit helps us in our weakness. We do not know what we ought to pray for, but the Spirit himself intercedes for us" (Romans 8:26). Among the results of Spirit-filled living are love, joy, and peace (Galatians 5:22)—what better equipment for enduring a storm?

The fact that the Spirit indwells us does not mean that we need not make preparation for the storms ourselves. We all need to get in shape spiritually so that when tested, we are resilient, strong, full of faith. How can we do this?

• *Fill your mind with the Word.* Then the Holy Spirit can remind you of the most-needed words at the most desperate times.

• *Practice committing your "small" problems to God.* If you can't trust God with the past-due bills, your daughter's sniffles, or an important interview, how can you trust Him when a loved one dies suddenly, you lose your job, or a fire destroys your home? Faith is like anything else: You get better with practice. So start trusting today, and expect God's faithfulness.

• *Begin a prayer journal.* This creates a wonderful faith tool. As you list your prayer requests, and eventually their answers, you will have a tangible record of God's goodness and His reliability. You can turn to this book again and again to see how close God stays to you.

• *Pray that God will prepare you.* Consider that you may encounter unexpected hazards and seek God's strength for those times. "A wicked man puts up a bold front, but an upright man gives thought to his ways" (Proverbs 21:29).

I have lived through a number of natural disasters, potential hazards, and life-threatening accidents. When I relate my narrow escapes to people, the first thing they often say is, "You sure were lucky!" But I don't believe in luck—I believe in God's faithfulness! I had prepared for these disasters by building my faith. So when the earth quaked, I had a powerful pillar to lean upon. And God's Spirit replaced my human response with His supernatural one—a welcome shelter in the midst of a storm.

> *The great crises of life are not, I think, necessarily those*
> *which are in themselves the hardest to bear, but those*
> *for which we are least prepared.*
>
> MARY ADAMS

Promise: The trusting heart will know peace. "In repentance and rest is your salvation, in quietness and trust is your strength" (Isaiah 30:15).

How do we find rest when our world is topsy-turvy—how do we settle our anxious thoughts when calamity strikes? Again, practice is the key. Robert Louis Stevenson wrote, "Quiet minds cannot be perplexed or frightened, but go on in fortune or misfortune at their own private pace, like a clock during a thunderstorm." Use these steps to create a quiet, steadfast mind.

• *Think upon the Savior and all He does for you day by day.* "Fix your thoughts on Jesus, the apostle and high priest whom we confess…. Christ is faithful as a son over God's house. And we are his house, if we hold on to our courage and the hope of which we boast" (Hebrews 3:1, 6).

• *Remember the Lord's faithfulness to you in the past.* "Yet this I call to mind and therefore I have hope: Because of the LORD's great love we are not consumed, for his compassions never fail. They are new every morning; great is your faithfulness" (Lamentations 3:21–23).

• *Trust that God will bring His help to you.* "The LORD is good to those whose hope is in him, to the one who seeks him…. Though he brings grief, he will show compassion, so great is his unfailing love. For he does not willingly bring affliction or grief to the children of men" (Lamentations 3:25, 32–33).

• *-Repent of panic and faithlessness—embrace peace.* "He must turn from evil and do good; he must seek peace and pursue it. For the eyes of the Lord are on the righteous and his ears are attentive to their prayer" (1 Peter 3:11–12).

Make yourselves nests of pleasant thoughts.
None of us yet know, for none of us have been taught in early youth,
what fairy palaces we may build of beautiful thought—proof
against all adversity.
Bright fancies, satisfied memories, noble histories, faithful sayings,
treasure-houses of precious and restful thoughts, which care cannot
disturb, nor pain make gloomy, nor poverty take away from us—houses
built without hands, for our souls to live in.
JOHN RUSKIN

CONCLUSION: SOMETHING BETTER IS COMING

Does pain mar your hope today? Are you disheartened by the darkness, the relentless assault of wind and rain? Does the storm feel like more than you can cope with, let alone rise above? Friend, here is good news: You are just the person God can strengthen. Who needs peace but the war-torn? Who needs help but the powerless? Who needs restoration but the ruined?

You are in a prime position to see the Lord of heaven work. Watch for Him. Pray for His power. Expect His help. You never know what is on the other side of a momentary terror. The late minister H. C. Trumbull once told the true story of a man who had lost his home and everything he owned in a devastating flood. Discouraged beyond compare, the man stood on the riverbank after the water had subsided and wept as he surveyed his losses. His house was gone; his barn and livestock had disappeared.

Then suddenly, in the distance, he caught sight of something shining across the bank that the waters had washed bare. "It can't be—but it looks like gold," he said in wonder.

Friend, it *was* gold…the flood that had taken everything from him also made him rich. The losses he had suffered were nothing compared to the riches he gained!

How many times has God brought something wonderful out of our greatest disappointment, sorrow, or loss? While God does not promise a trouble-free life, He does promise His presence—and it will be enough.

The lowest ebb is the turn of the tide.
HENRY WADSWORTH LONGFELLOW

CHAPTER SIX

A MATTER OF LIFE AND DEATH

*Everyone who is born holds dual citizenship,
in the kingdom of the well and in the kingdom of the sick.
Although we all prefer to use only the good passport, sooner or later
each of us is obliged, at least for a spell, to identify ourselves
as citizens of that other place.*

SUSAN SONTAG

Sickness is one of the threads that bind humanity together. Every one of us had or will at some point have some sort of "dis-ease" of the body. Because we are temporal beings, we all endure the slow decay of the human receptacle we live in. This decay begins for some people in youth; others, in midlife; and some, not until they are elderly.

One of the great mysteries of life is why some folks have been given seemingly defective bodies—ones that easily acquire illness, resist medication, and are unable to function normally. This experience is "the sickness that stays," chronic illness. There are also those persons who must bear up under sudden, tragic diagnoses and the terror of fast-approaching death. In whatever form it manifests itself, let's admit it: Sickness is a real pain.

It is also an opportunity, a chance to experience in fresh, unusual ways, God's care, His health, and His peace. Even when our bodies are distressed, our spirits can be calmed. The only way to experience a true sense of serenity in the midst of this storm is to take shelter in the Father's Word. His promises will equip us to stand when we ache, to smile when we hurt, and to hope when everything looks dismal.

GOD IS THE KEEPER OF THE SPIRIT

Key Promise: "My help and glory are in God—granite-strength and safe-harbor-God—so trust him absolutely, people; lay your lives on the line for him. God is a safe place to be" (Psalm 62:7–8, *The Message*).

Perhaps you sat in that uncomfortable chair in the doctor's office recently while awaiting test results. You know the edgy anxiety, the rush of fear. The clock ticks too loudly in the room, reminding you that life is passing even as you sit there. You wonder which is worse, wondering or knowing. At the same time you both dread and crave the doctor's prognosis. You know your life is about to change forever. *You have cancer. It's malignant. Chemotherapy. Radiation. Surgery. Go home and get your house in order.* Your thoughts are full of ideas you do not want to think about, words that echo so loudly you want to run from the room screaming.

I have been in that seat. For several days I lived in fear that my life was coming to an end. The odds terrified me. I clearly remember the sharp stabs of panic that afflicted me while I waited for the results of a second test. To be honest, I did not possess the faith I needed in that situation. I spent a tortured weekend crying buckets of tears and struggling to stay busy. I called several friends and begged them to pray, which terrified them also. It was an awful time.

I am one of the lucky ones. The results of my second test came back clear. But since that close call, I have never been the same. I know the inside, outside, top, and bottom of this storm; and I know how horrifying a place it can be. Although I have not dealt with chronic or terminal illness, I have tasted the acidic edge of it. I have dug deep for promises to cling to, and I have seen what God can do.

The main gift God brings in the midst of illness is healing—although it isn't necessarily healing of the body. It is the spirit that God seems interested in foremost. And it is primarily the spirit He speaks to through His promises. Friend, if you are ill and full of despair, let God's promises fill you with something better, Himself. I hope His healing comes to you in your body, but also in your spirit, because your spirit is what lasts.

Norman Vincent Peale wrote some enormously comforting words for when we face death; these words might also be applied to times when we face illness. He likens the process of dying to that of being born:

> An infant, snuggled up under the mother's heart in the pre-natal days, is surrounded by warmth and protection. If he could reason, the baby might say, "I don't want to be born; I don't want to go out of this world into that other world. I am happy here; I am afraid of birth."
>
> In his pre-natal existence, he might regard birth as we do death, as the end of one certain experience and the beginning of another uncertain one. Then he is born. Looking down at him is the kindest and sweetest face in the world. He is cuddled in his mother's loving arms. There he is held and protected, fed and loved. God made it that way.
>
> So after many years, when a man comes to die, need he be terrified at the prospect of death—or, if you please, of another birth? Should he fear to pass from this world into the next? If he had love and protection when first he came to this earth, may he not assume he will have the same as he enters the next life? Can we not trust the same God to take care of us in death as He did in birth? Will His attribute of love so quickly change? It would not be like Him.[1]

I believe the first thing we should do after becoming ill is to follow the biblical mandates—ask others to pray, and seek the Lord's healing (James 5:14–15). As we await God's response, we should also look to the Lord for the restoration of our spirits—the soothing that is supernatural. Come meet some friends who have sought and found God's faithfulness even when illness racked—or threatened—their lives. Like them, you too may say, "Unless the LORD had given me help, I would soon have dwelt in the silence of death. When I said, 'My foot is slipping,' your love, O LORD, supported me. When anxiety was great within me, your consolation brought joy to my soul" (Psalm 94:17–19).

> *Courage conquers all things; it even gives strength to the body.*
> OVID

BRUISED BUT NOT BROKEN

My dear friend Kim poignantly shared with me her battle against anorexia, a common killer these days. Her story depicts both the misery of disease and the beauty of God's deliverance.

How do I explain anorexia? It's like a carnival mirror that distorts your image. No matter what you do or how thin you become, your shape is still grossly exaggerated in your mind. The only way out is to receive new sight.

It started for me at the age of sixteen. It was a traumatic time: My mother had recently been diagnosed with terminal cancer. My world was sliding downward, and I didn't know how to make it stop. When a person loses her balance, the natural inclination is to grab on to something. But in the midst of this surreal and frightening storm, I felt helpless. I could find nothing to stop my slide. I decided, almost subconsciously, to take control of the only thing I could, my body. I began to eat less. Watching the pounds drop away made me feel powerful.

When I was hungry, I suppressed the desire to eat. When other people invited me to eat, I told them that I had already eaten. After a while, the pain in my stomach subsided and the feeling of emptiness that replaced it became my normal state of being. It just felt right. One can of tuna a day and all the diet soda I could drink allowed me to attain the desired weight. At five feet six inches tall, I weighed only ninety-three pounds. When my weight fluctuated due to water gain each month, I panicked. More starvation: Nothing but a dry baked potato a day, and all was well in my world.

Several years went by as I continued this bizarre ritual of starvation and denial. The cramping in my muscles and the tremors in my hands had people concerned that I was a drug abuser, but the symptoms were merely by-products of a nervous system in agony. My ribs were now visible through my chest and my hipbones protruded through my clothes. The real test lay in making certain that my inner thighs didn't touch. I wanted to have no breasts, no buttocks, no curves of any sort. I was queen of my domain, and I resolved to stay that way. When people commented on my weight, my reply was always the same: "I just have a fast metabolism." Lying had become a way of life.

One day I choked on a tortilla chip in a restaurant. I was too embarrassed to tell my friends that I hadn't eaten in three days and that my throat muscles had forgotten how to swallow. If people found out that I was deathly afraid of putting food in my mouth, they might think something was wrong with me. But as far as I was concerned, there wasn't. I just liked being thin. Thin was beautiful. I felt like a strong person, able to exercise amazing self-discipline.

It's funny what the body will do to get your attention. As my blood pressure dropped steadily, I would sometimes faint just getting out of bed. Heart arrhythmia, chest pains, insomnia, hypoglycemia, staggered breathing, internal tremors, muscle cramps, blurred vision, mental lethargy, night sweats, excessive bruising—these were all pleas from my tired body. But it didn't matter. My eyes still saw a fat girl in the mirror, and staying thin was all I could think about. It was what I had become—malnourished, dehydrated, and anemic. I made several emergency room visits, but my perspective didn't change.

Incredibly, I survived this affliction for thirty-five years. Some might say that I was very lucky. I say that it was nothing short of miraculous. Anorexia almost took my life. But our God is a God of restoration.

If it weren't for several amazing Christian women in my life, I wouldn't be here to tell you this story. They placed me before the throne of God daily, and interceded for me when I couldn't pray for myself. There were days when I wondered, *How long would it take my heart to stop beating if I just didn't eat again?* The thought of dying was sometimes easier than the thought of continuing on. As my strength continued to ebb, these women were faithful in holding me up. When a walk through the grocery store left me panicked, they were praying. When the mere idea of opening the refrigerator door reduced me to tears, they were praying. When I sat on the couch crying instead of fixing my next meal, they supplied the encouragement to make it through. Because of their persistence, I was eventually delivered.

I humbly report that I have been in remission for four years now. I weigh 120 pounds, and I'm stronger now than I have ever been. God is the ultimate physician; He healed me from more than just an eating disorder. He gave me a new life and the tools to help other girls with the same devastating disease. I thank those patient, steadfast prayer warriors who never quit standing on His promises.

Kim's story lends a wise point: When you can't help yourself, get others to help. When you can no longer pray or hope, someone is available to do these things for you. Let them minister to you, intercede for you, and bring your distress before the Father. He has provided other believers to be tangible sources of His care—to be umbrellas for you when the rains come.

Life's sharpest rapture is the surcease of pain.
EMMA LAZARUS

WHEN THE PAIN ISN'T PHYSICAL

When I share this episode of my life with friends, they are always stunned. "You, depressed? I don't believe it!" People are always telling me that I have such a positive outlook, so much faith and trust in my heavenly Father, that surely I could never be brought down. But there was a time when I was mired in darkness. At the time, many of my friends didn't know about it because I was ashamed. Those who did know said things like, "Have faith! This, too, shall pass." But it didn't.

Depression is a storm that leaves one feeling forsaken, afraid, and unequipped to fix the situation. I am living proof that God is not overwhelmed by this storm—even in this terrifying place, His love is strong and real. And when He heals anew, it's always better than before. The lessons I learned while in the gloom provided me with a strong shield of faith. Here is my story.

The dark cloud gathered over my head during what should have been a celebration: the birth of my child.

Medicated with painkillers and hooked up to an IV, I peered foggily around my hospital room. It was filled with flowers, and the hospital aide came in with another cartful. "For you!" she crowed cheerfully. But even the good wishes of my many friends around the country did not brighten my mood. I had been taken over by a strange darkness.

I had delivered a healthy baby girl by cesarean section just a few hours before. I was surrounded by family and friends. This was supposed to be one of the happiest days of my life, but I could feel within myself that it had become one of the worst.

I felt as though I had been sawed in two, and I assumed that my pervading sorrow was due to this post-surgery pain. My mind swam with hopeless thoughts, and I wondered when I would begin to experience the joy of motherhood.

A nurse entered the room, my new daughter in her arms. "Here's your sweet baby, honey."

I turned my head away. "I can't hold her now."

The nurse was shocked. "You have to feed your baby!"

I began to cry. I didn't want to feed my baby. Fortunately, the nurse suggested that my husband give our daughter a bottle of water. Guilt slowly began to creep in, bringing with it more darkness.

That evening more than fifty visitors descended upon us. They came to welcome our new baby into the world. The hospital room took on a party atmosphere; trying desperately to keep a smile pasted on my face, I felt as though I were attending a costume ball. Fortunately, the doctor dropped by and, sensing my discomfort, placed a No Visitors sign on my door, which eventually dispersed my friends and family.

Finally left alone, I let the tears flow. I cried out to God, but He was silent.

"You'll feel better in a few days," my doctor assured me the next morning. But he was wrong. I did not feel better in a few days, or in a few weeks, or in a few months. I was a victim of the "baby blues," also known as acute postpartum depression. It seemed as though nothing could lift the dark cloud that hovered over me, not even my repeated cries to God.

Not only was I dealing with severe depression; I was consumed with guilt because I was not the happy new mother that everyone expected me to be.

"Having a baby is the greatest experience you'll ever have!" a friend said. Another insisted, "Being a mother is the most fulfilling thing in life." "Women are so blessed to have the children," I was told. "Motherhood is heavenly," confided my neighbor, who had given birth a few weeks after me.

I held my hands over my ears as their comments rang inside my head. I felt like I was in hell. Every morning when I awoke I was terrified at the thought of trying to survive another dark day. I literally began counting the hours until I could escape each night to the haven of sleep.

I went through the motions of caring for my baby, but I withdrew further and further from everyone. Fear that someone might notice my despair horrified me. I had never encountered anyone with this ailment. I read all of the pregnancy and birth books that I could get my hands on, but I found only a few short paragraphs referencing postpartum depression. In every case, the author assured me that my depression would lift within a couple of months.

But it didn't. Anxiety joined depression, and the two began to take over my life. As I went about my tasks and responsibilities, I would intone dully, "I can do all things through Christ who strengthens me" (Philippians 4:13, NKJV). I maintained a dim hope in the Lord, although I could neither see nor feel His presence.

At my checkup I attempted to tell my doctor what I was feeling, and he encouraged me to join a mother-and-child play group. The play group only served to depress me more, since all of the young mothers were thrilled with the joys of parenting.

I became a prisoner in my home. My husband began to suspect that I wasn't enjoying new motherhood, although I did my best to hide my feelings. It upset him when I began refusing to accompany him to social functions. "I don't want to leave the baby," I lied.

My mother and I spent hours on the phone. Although she tried to encourage me, there was no way she could understand; raising babies had been one of the great joys of her life. "We'll just keep praying, and I'm sure this will pass," she said.

I kept a notebook of God's promises, and although I drew strength from His Word, I did not find the healing I sought. I wondered, *Will I be afflicted like Paul, with this thorn of depression in my side forever? Is God's grace sufficient for me?* I counseled with my pastor, who explained that life is full of problems, even for Christians. I didn't want to hear this. I had been raised to believe that if you acted the right way and made the right choices, everything would turn out okay. Now I was being told, "This is life." I knew that I couldn't spend the rest of my days this way.

One year after giving birth to Megan, I finally dialed 9-1-1, and my husband took me to the emergency room. At long last, I began receiving the help I needed.

A few months later I began taking proper medication and attending weekly therapy sessions. A seed of hope sprang within me; I was *working* on the problem. I knew that God had provided this opportunity, and for the first time I sensed that He was still acting on my behalf.

It took more than two years for my depression to lift fully. Although I stood firmly on God's healing promises, my affliction did not dissolve miraculously. The meticulous process involved finding the right medication for my hormonal imbalance and the right therapy to help me resolve lingering doubts and fears. Healing unfolded gradually, in stages.

Today I can say that my experience with severe depression served a purpose in my life. It led me back into a deep, intense study of God's Word, and for this I will be eternally grateful. Sometimes I long for a little more of the time that I spent with the Lord and His Word during my illness. The growth I experienced in those last two years, as medication and therapy gradually assuaged my depression, was truly a miracle. God used that dark time in my life to equip me with the tools I would need to fulfill His plan and purpose in my life. Illness is a very lonely, disheartening storm, and I now know how to relate to women who struggle with it.

Friend, if you suffer from chronic feelings of despair, please seek immediate help from both your heavenly Father and from health-care professionals. Do not suffer in silence. Do not berate yourself for a lack of faith. God understands. Depression is an illness and is often indicative of a chemical imbalance—something that can be treated. Use the resources God has provided to escape from this dark place; He will empower your steps.

> *Whenever evil befall us, we ought to ask ourselves,*
> *after the first suffering, how we can turn it into good.*
> *So shall we take occasion, from one bitter root,*
> *to raise perhaps many flowers.*
> LEIGH HUNT

SICKNESS: A BRIDGE TO GOD

My dear friend and spiritual mentor, Carolynn Guthrie Barela, has a testimony that illustrates how God deals with us as individuals and how He sometimes uses unusual means to get our attention.

It was a perfectly beautiful Sunday afternoon. My husband and I were out sailing on the sparkling waters of Lake Ponchatrain in New Orleans. This was a favorite outing for our family. After sailing for a couple of hours, I unexpectedly doubled over in excruciating pain from my waist down. I began to panic as I lost all feeling in my lower extremities. Minutes later, our glorious afternoon dissolved as I was rushed to the emergency room by ambulance, sirens wailing and lights flashing.

After an extensive examination, the doctors shook their heads, unable to make a conclusive diagnosis. They finally performed a biopsy on some suspicious lymph nodes and left me to ponder my fate.

I lay unable to move in my hospital bed. Never before had I been so aware of my estrangement from God. I needed Him now more than ever, but I had to admit that other than my children's christenings, I had not been in a church or given God much thought for more than thirteen years.

A doctor entered my room to give me the results of an initial test. "Carolynn, the pathology doesn't look good, but the final report won't be back until tomorrow."

"Is it cancer?" I whispered, afraid to voice the words too loudly.

"We don't know. We'll have to wait and see what develops."

"But will I be able to walk again?" I asked softly.

"It looks like the paralysis could very well be permanent," he said as he left.

With those hopeless words, the doctor left me alone with my thoughts. Nurses came in every few hours to turn my body in order to prevent the onset of pneumonia. Close to midnight, too full of frantic thought to rest, I began to despair. I stared at the crucifix on the wall and began to talk to Jesus. *Why in the world did You give me five children if I am going to have to raise them from a wheelchair?* I cried out.

Instantly I remembered the words of David: "He maketh me to lie down in green pastures.... He restoreth my soul" (Psalm 23:2–3, KJV).

I kept praying: *Lord, I have a full life, everything money can buy, and five wonderful children. But I was too busy for You, and now I need You. Please help me!*

An incredible peace enveloped me. It was as though the Lord had taken me in His arms. All my fears and worries melted away as I fell asleep.

At two in the morning I woke up. I could move! I was stunned. All of the feeling had come back into my body. I sat up just as the nurses were entering the room to turn me. "What did you do?" one of them asked incredulously.

"God has totally healed me!" I squealed, dangling my legs over the side of the hospital bed.

The next morning my doctor came in and said, "Carolynn, they called to tell me that you were able to move your legs again. The pathologist is perplexed, too, because your tissue looks unhealthy, but under the microscope there's no sign of disease." He paused, then asked matter of factly, "Do you believe in God?"

I smiled. "Funny you should ask me that."

"Well, do you?" he asked persistently.

I shared about my miraculous encounter, but confessed that until the previous night I had known only of God's existence; I hadn't known Him.

The doctor admitted that my altered physical state was incredible, but insisted that he would need to monitor me for a few more days, to make certain that nothing was wrong. His concerns didn't faze me. Although I couldn't explain it, I knew that Jesus had healed me the night before.

A few days later I left the hospital. My diagnosis had been inconclusive, but my body felt fine!

Charles, a houseguest from Houston, arrived at our home. He was surprised to learn of my hospitalization and confessed that he had planned to share the Lord with me during his visit. We were awed when we realized that the Sunday I suffered the paralysis was the same Sunday his church was fervently praying for my salvation. Something was definitely happening.

Charles was a brilliant man, someone I respected and enjoyed debating on every subject from politics to Hollywood. When the conversation turned to God, we talked until five in the morning. He got out his Bible, and we went over the Scriptures I didn't understand and the ones that really bothered me. We had a great visit, and Charles returned to Houston.

Close to noon the next day, I was sitting in a chair feeding my baby a bottle. Suddenly I began to weep. Tears were pretty unusual for me. I was a tough lady, an organized perfectionist who rarely got her feathers ruffled. I could handle five children, a high-maintenance husband, and a large, busy household without batting an eyelash. But today I couldn't stop crying. I finished feeding my baby and put her back in bed. When I returned to my room, I knelt beside my bed and began to pray: *God, if you are really there, Charles tells me that I need to be born again. But I don't know anything about You, Lord, not even how to love You. Please give me wisdom. That's all I'm asking.*

The next day when I went to the mailbox, I found a package. It was a Living Bible. I had never owned a Bible before, and I held it close to my chest. I suddenly longed for this God I did not know. I looked up to heaven and said, *Oh, God, this is about You,* and opened it up. "I do not pray that you will destroy my enemies, I only pray for wisdom," Solomon wrote (see 1 Kings 3:9–12). "Because you have asked for this and not to destroy your enemies, I give you wisdom and I give you everything else."

I knew that God was speaking directly to me. I had prayed for wisdom, and He had led me directly to His Word! Not only was He giving me wisdom, He was giving me everything He offers His children: forgiveness, joy, love, and much more!

When I remembered my prayer request and saw God's answer, I realized that God was seeking me—acting on my behalf to get me to seek Him. My temporary paralysis, my conversation with Him in the hospital, Charles's wise words, the prayers of his church family, and the way my prayer echoed Solomon's in the Bible all added up to one thing: Love was wooing me. I accepted the Lord with all my heart, soul, and mind that day, and I have walked with Him ever since—on steady, completely healed legs, I might add!

In Carolynn's case, both her spirit and her body were restored to health. While this doesn't happen for everyone, it teaches us a lesson about the reality of God's mercy. He does what He needs to in order to get our attention. He wants each of us so much that He designs the means to reach us. For Carolynn, it was a terrifying illness and a friend's fervent prayer. What will it be for you?

I thank God for my handicaps, for, through them,
I have found myself, my work, and my God.

HELEN KELLER

PROMISES TO STAND ON

Promise: God is your source for contentment in the midst of pain. "You will keep in perfect peace him whose mind is steadfast, because he trusts in you. Trust in the LORD forever, for the LORD, the LORD, is the Rock eternal" (Isaiah 26:3–4).

Illness creates isolation. Is anything lonelier than the affliction of a malady that causes pain, keeps you from your work and your family, and refuses to go away? It affects your mind and your body. Yet the sun still shines—which seems unjust when you feel lousy—and life around you continues. You begin to feel incapable and unneeded. How do you cope with this slow storm?

You can turn to the One who is able to overcome what overwhelms you. As you follow doctors' orders and wise counsel, seek the Lord's physical touch of wholeness as well as His emotional support. Let Him supply the peace and understanding you can't muster. Isaiah wrote that God would keep in perfect peace the one whose mind was fixed on trust in Him. Your role is to set your eyes on His goodness—to trust in it even when you don't see it—and to let Him fill you with His rest. Only He can do that! So look to Him. Cry out, and wait for His answer. Ask loved ones to pray, as well. The Lord says that those who seek Him, find Him— "...when you seek me with all your heart" (Jeremiah 29:13).

> *You don't get ulcers from what you eat.*
> *You get them from what's eating you.*
> VICKI BAUM

Promise: God is with you every step of the way. "This God is our God for ever and ever; he will be our guide even to the end" (Psalm 48:14).

Illness may attack your body, but it doesn't have to consume your spirit. Try these activities as "preventative medicine" for a healthy soul:

- Keep a notebook of healing Scriptures to pray during your illness. Search the Bible for them. Here are a couple to get you started: "Heal me, O LORD, and I shall be healed; save me, and I shall be saved, for You are my praise" (Jeremiah 17:14, NKJV). "You are my hiding place and my shield; I hope in Your word" (Psalm 119:114, NKJV).
- Pray often. "Evening and morning and at noon I will pray, and cry aloud, and He shall hear my voice" (Psalm 55:17, NKJV).
- If it is physically possible, do a good deed every day (or week) for someone else. A friend of mine, who was recently diagnosed with leukemia, began to tutor underprivileged children. She found herself deeply enriched through this act of service. It is truly in giving that we receive.
- For extra encouragement, read books by others who have struggled with illness. You may better learn how to bear your burden by hearing how others bore theirs.

- Seek peace in all you do. Mend relationships; settle inner conflicts; resolve old issues. "A heart at peace gives life to the body, but envy rots the bones" (Proverbs 14:30).

- Laugh! Research by the late physician Norman Cousins shows that sick people actually improve when they watch funny movies. Rent some comical films, read amusing books, hang out with fun friends.

- Spend time praising God. This keeps your eyes focused on the good things He is doing and on the Father Himself: "I will praise the LORD, who counsels me; even at night my heart instructs me. I have set the LORD always before me. Because he is at my right hand, I will not be shaken" (Psalm 16:7–8).

- Live in the present. Don't dwell on the past or worry about the future. Deal with each moment as it comes. Jesus said, "Do not worry about tomorrow, for tomorrow will worry about itself. Each day has enough trouble of its own" (Matthew 6:34).

- Spend time thinking about what is unseen but eternal. This is healthy advice whether you are ill or not! Read books concerning what the Father has prepared for you (I suggest *Heaven: Your Real Home* by Joni Eareckson Tada). "We know that if the earthly tent we live in is destroyed, we have a building from God, an eternal house in heaven, not built by human hands" (2 Corinthians 5:1).

A Bible falling apart usually belongs to someone who isn't.
MY GRANDMOTHER HUEY

CONCLUSION:
NOTHING CAN DESTROY GOD'S PLAN

Does suffering weigh you down today? Are you heavy-laden with sorrow, weary from wondering when this will end? Our physical and emotional sides are so intertwined that if one is strained, the other suffers as well. If illness has shackled you, no doubt you feel the effects in your mood, your outlook, and your attitude.

When feelings dictate doom, remember that God is still on His throne. He is still in charge of life and death—including yours. And He is still at work, making something beautiful out of something dark and dreadful. Appearances are not everything—in fact, they constitute very little. Consider past ways in which hindsight revealed God's actions, after you suspected He was just being silent. Remember that He knows no weariness, and that He is never dissuaded from His task or His love. Remember and hope.

Let this story encourage you.

A boy named Will was born with neurological damage. It affected his motor skills, and when he was three months old, his doctors sadly told his parents that the boy would never walk. His mother, a friend of mine, refused to accept this, and she enlisted me to help pray. I did so, inserting his name in a verse that I repeated to the Lord: "Will, who hopes in the Lord, will renew his strength. Will will soar on wings like eagles; Will will run and not grow weary, Will will walk and not be faint" (see Isaiah 40:31). We believed in better things for this little boy.

Two years later on Christmas Day, my friend called with the joyous news, "Will is walking!" He took a little longer than most kids, but he had more to overcome than they did. God produced something wonderful in the midst of Will's physical malady. He did not remove Will's handicap, but He limited its effect. He rewarded our faith, and He showed us His love.

I pray that He does the same for you today. Friend, put your faith in the Father. Pray for Him to reveal His light and His love in this long, windy storm.

We shall be made truly wise if we be made content;
content, too, not only with what we can understand, but
content with what we do not understand—the habit of mind
which theologians call, and rightly, faith in God.

CHARLES KINGSLEY

CHAPTER SEVEN

Attention, Mothers: This Is Only a Test!

Children in a family are like flowers in a bouquet:
There's always one determined to face in an opposite direction
from the way the arranger desires.

MARCELENE COX

*D*id you read our opening quote with the eyes of understanding?

The mother who struggles with a wayward child experiences deep frustration. You are tormented by nagging questions: *Where did I go wrong? How could I have prevented this? How can I fix the mess my child is in?* You feel your child's failures and losses keenly. You may feel the responsibility to mend your child's wrongs, a task far beyond your powers. Disturbing emotions rumble within you: embarrassment, fear, anger, pain.

A wayward child is a particularly heart-wrenching storm. To make matters worse, many a mother bases her self-esteem on the behavioral pattern of her child. *If Tommy performs well, I am a wonderful parent.* But if he blows it—hurts someone, errs in a public way, earns long-lasting punishment—you feel as though you have failed. Then there is the aspect of spiritual failure: As a Christian, you take the role of godly instructor seriously. When your child refuses to serve God, you hang your head before the Creator and despair.

Weary mother, good news: You are equipped to weather this

storm. Not only do you have wise instruction at your fingertips, you have companionship. God the Father understands the difficulties encountered in raising a rebellious child, and He will stand with you through the howling winds of this storm. Lean on His promises, and reach for His hand in the darkness.

GOD'S POWER IS LIMITLESS

Key Promise: "God can do anything, you know—far more than you could ever imagine or guess or request in your wildest dreams! He does it not by pushing us around but by working within us, his Spirit deeply and gently within us" (Ephesians 3:20, *The Message*).

Parenting tribulation is a storm I have personally endured. Believe me, it wasn't for lack of effort. I began praying for my daughter the moment I found out that I was pregnant. She attended Bible studies with me from six weeks on. She was steeped in prayer and in Scripture. In fact, Meg probably rates up there with the top one hundred kids ever prayed for. With all that intercession and instruction and spiritual investment, I felt comfortable assuming that Meg would turn out to be a perfect child. Was I in for a surprise!

I should have sensed that I was headed for battle during the delivery. A textbook labor made a downward spiral when Meg turned herself one hundred eighty degrees into a breech position. This eliminated the option of natural childbirth.

I told my doctor that I wasn't going to have a cesarean section. He told me I was. As they wheeled me into the delivery room, I realized that I was experiencing my first battle with my daughter. She won.

Congratulations, Mom! You are now the parent of a strong-willed child!

It may have been the first battle, but it certainly wasn't the last. For reasons beyond my understanding, my beloved daughter rebelled during her teen years. She not only refused to heed my guidance; she also refused to acknowledge God's authority in her life. She made painful decisions, chose damaging friendships, and suffered many losses. As her mother, I also suffered. I felt deep disappointment in myself and longed to restore my relationship with her; I wondered how I could face God as a failed parent. Those were miserable, dark days. The storm clouds rode low around my heart, and I wondered how we would survive.

A pivotal meeting turned me from storm victim to standing victor. My husband and I finally consulted a former youth pastor about Meg's problems. We told him everything. We listed every painful choice Meg had made, including the ones we would have preferred to keep secret. Frankly, we expected him to be shocked. Instead he was calm, relaxed, even matter of fact. "It doesn't matter," he told us.

Surprised, I said, "I don't understand."

"The only thing that really matters is your daughter's salvation." He explained that her behavior, her choices, her failures, her lifestyle—none of it was all that important. We were focusing on Meg's outward behavior when we should be focusing on her spiritual needs. It was a watershed realization.

Something amazing happened to me at that moment: The burden fell away. I stopped worrying. I stopped trying to fix everything. My husband and I committed to putting Meg's actions aside—not to give our approval of them, but to see them as secondary—and to fixing our eyes on Jesus. After all, He is the Savior. I saw for the first time that just as only God could save my daughter's soul, only He could save her life on earth as well. Though Meg had accepted Jesus as her Savior at a young age and didn't walk with Him now, He was active in her life. He could do all that I, as a parent, couldn't. His power was perfect and limitless.

I have since found comfort in the fact that God has a plan for Meg's life and that He alone can weave the pieces together in a beautiful way. Everything she has experienced will contribute to that plan, and God will use all of her successes and failures to fulfill His purpose for her. He will use every step she has taken for His glory and her good—I believe this.

I know as well that my job as a mother is limited. All that I was able to do, I did. Today my biggest contributions to Meg's life are my constant prayers and my unconditional love. I keep my eyes on Jesus and continue to focus on the positives. I have stopped trying to control, correct, and command. I relinquish my daughter to the perfect, loving, powerful care of my Father. That's what grace lets us do.

Meg is still on her own journey of discovery. Though some of her choices are not yet what I hope for, I know that God is at work in her life. She is a wonderful girl: a hard worker who helps pay for her school expenses, a great student, and a champion of social issues. She has an enormous heart of compassion. Though she attends church only on Christmas and Easter, she recently told me that she is praying every day. She even calls to ask me to pray with her concerning important decisions and for friends. I'm still standing on the promises, waiting for God to weave all the threads of Meg's life into a beautiful tapestry—I know He is untangling them at this very minute! I have resisted the temptation to help God out a little by cutting a few mangled threads. I wait in hope.

You moms who have been in my shoes know how it is. You nod in empathy when I confess that it has been a long, hard road. Occasionally, I'm tempted to fret and have to stop and remember that fixing the situation is not God's calling for me. Sometimes I'm surprised to find myself still standing. It is only by God's grace that I am—it's only because of His promises that I can sleep at night. Friend, come meet some parents who understand your pain. See how they staggered, struggled, and eventually stood—all because God was faithful to His promises.

For peace of mind, resign as general manager of the universe.
ANONYMOUS

WHEN GOD SPOKE

For those of you who are braving the storm of drug or alcohol abuse with your child, Karen's inspirational story can help you to see the sun shining through the dark clouds.

It is a frightening place for a mother to be: full of love for her child, yet shocked and horrified at his lifestyle. Like many other parents, my husband and I lived in fear daily: afraid that our son would never be set free from his drug addiction, afraid that his dangerous habit would one day claim his life. Yet through God's grace we learned to hate the sin and yet love the sinner.

When Ron was just a teenager, we sent him to several costly rehabilitation centers. We provided him with the best-trained counselors we could find. We spent almost every dime we earned on Ron's treatment, which often forced our other children to make enormous sacrifices so that their brother could be taken care of. My husband and I could not have lived with ourselves if we had not taken every possible step to try to save our son.

When Ron reached the age of adulthood, it became obvious that he had fallen back into drug use. Despite the fact that we continued to hope, pray, and believe that we could somehow help him, the realization dawned that it was time to set some serious boundaries. We decided to stop all contact with our son. We closed our home, our pocketbooks, and our hearts to him.

My head said that this extreme of an action was necessary, but my heart told me otherwise. I tossed and turned nightly, wondering if we were being too harsh. Was our son safe? Was he cold or hungry? Did he have a place to sleep? Not knowing tormented me. Yet we believed it was the only way our son would ever be healed.

I finally told my husband that I didn't feel right about not even accepting our son's phone calls.

"That's because you're his mother," he told me gently.

"Jesus was pretty tough on the prostitutes and the tax collectors," I pointed out, "but he still hung out with them."

I knew that my husband was also experiencing doubt, but he was committed to sticking with our decision. No one had ever told us it would be easy.

After an especially long and sleepless night, I began to pace the floor and cry out to the Lord. In the midst of my cries, the Lord spoke to my heart. The next morning I shared the revelation that He had given me. "We all have sins and fall short of God's glory, but God invites us *all* into His family."

My husband softened at these words. He left to find our son and tell him that we forgave him, that he was welcome in our home as long as he wasn't high.

Ron began to visit us again. Like any addict, at times he was clean and at other times we were forced to turn him away. Having to refuse him entrance into our home always broke our hearts—especially on one particularly cold, snowy Christmas morning when our entire family had gathered to celebrate the holiday.

Through God's promises I was able to remain standing, even through the trials and disappointments. I staked my hope on 2 Corinthians 5:17: "If anyone is in Christ, he is a new creation; the old has gone, the new has come." I knew that my son had been given a free will and was responsible for his own life. But I never gave up hoping that Ron would be set free of his addiction to drugs. And as I waited and hoped, I prayed.

One hot summer evening Ron showed up at our door, sober and freshly shaven. After dinner he announced that he had just gotten a job at the local hardware store.

"That's nice," I replied rather vaguely. Neither his father nor I were overly excited by the news, since Ron had taken dozens of jobs in the past, only to lose them during a drug binge.

"I've met a girl, too," he added, grinning.

Again his father and I struggled to muster enthusiasm, despite the fact that Ron was known for changing girlfriends as often as he changed his socks. This was not uncommon behavior for a charming, handsome addict like our son.

It was to his next statement that we reacted in surprise:

"You'll be happy to know that she doesn't do drugs."

"Really?" I asked and bit my tongue to keep from adding, *Then why on earth is she interested in you?*

"I was wondering if I might invite her over for dinner tomorrow night," Ron said.

I shuddered. We had witnessed some really unpleasant scenes around the dinner table when Ron had brought drug friends into our home.

As though he could read my mind, Ron spoke up. "She's not like any of the others. You'll like her, Mom. Cindy's a Christian."

Out of sheer curiosity, Ralph and I agreed that Ron could invite Cindy to dinner at our home the following weekend. After her visit, I asked Ralph, "What do you think?"

"I feel sorry for her," he said softly. "She has no idea what she's getting into."

I nodded, wishing that things were different.

After several months, Cindy and Ron told us that they were thinking of getting married. I invited Cindy into the kitchen to help me with the dishes, and I began by questioning her faith: "How can you justify being unequally yoked with my son?"

"But Mrs. Green," she said in surprise, "Ron is a Christian."

"That may very well be true, but are you aware that he's also an addict?" I felt ashamed for turning on my son, who was clearly in love with this young woman.

She persisted. "But the Bible says, 'If anyone is in Christ, he is a new creation; the old has gone, the new has come!'" It was the very same verse that I had been clinging to, the verse that God had given me for Ron, the promise on which I had stood for so many years.

Cindy told me that Ron had recommitted his life to the Lord at her church, where he was attending a twelve-step program. Initially, they had stuck to a simple friendship; soon she began to see something special about him.

That night after they left, I told my husband the news. As Ron's parents, we had been hurt and disappointed too many times to get really excited. Yet as the months passed, we watched in awe as our son held down his job and managed to stay free of drugs.

After two years of sobriety, he and Cindy were married. A couple of years later, we cradled our granddaughter in our arms. We praised God not only for bringing our son back to us, but also for giving us a beautiful daughter-in-law and a healthy grandchild.

Ron recently confessed to us that he continues to live just one day at a time. Though he still struggles with a desire for drugs, he has—through God's grace and strength—been clean for several years.

"What was the turning point in your life?" my husband asked him.

"It was when you and Mom had a change of heart and welcomed me back home, in spite of my addiction."

I swallowed hard, silently praising God that we had listened to His voice. We had followed our hearts and allowed our prodigal son to return home, despite the professionals' advice to the contrary.

"Mom, your acceptance gave me a clear picture of God's unconditional love. That love drew me back into the body of Christ. God has provided me with a wife who also loves me unconditionally, and He provides the love and support that enables me to get through each day."

I wept tears of joy. Just as God deals with us individually, we must deal with situations according to God's leading. There are no clearly marked paths to follow; we must take God's hands through the storms and allow Him to lead us in His perfect way.

What a picture of courage this mother is to me! Faced with fear, confusion, and dilemmas she never asked for, she responded with heroic love and prayer. And it has made its mark in her son's life.

Like her, seek wisdom as you decide how to handle an addicted son or daughter. Talk to trusted, trained professionals and prayerfully consider their counsel. The Lord will show you the right thing to do. After all, families were His idea!

To pray is to open the door unto Jesus and admit Him into your distress.
Your helplessness is the very thing which opens wide the door
unto Him and gives Him access to all your needs.

O. HALLESBY

WHEN YOUR BABY HAS A BABY

One of the most devastating blows a mother can receive is to discover that her teenage daughter is pregnant. Truthfully, no mother ever knows how she will react to such a storm until it visits her personally. I believe this is why God warns Christians not to judge others; it is impossible to know what someone else is going through.

Emma trusted in God and chose His option. Through her example, you will see how God transformed a tragic situation. Let her story encourage you to believe in God's power.

When the doctor came out of the examining room, he was shaking his head. I knew instinctively that I did not want to hear the news he was about to deliver.

"Emma, your daughter is pregnant." My husband, Jim, had to support me as I collapsed.

We were Christians. Our daughter had been raised in the church, with the Lord at the center of our family's life. This was not supposed to happen to us. *Why, Lord?* Chloe was a lovely young woman; she made excellent grades. How could this have happened? To make matters even worse, when I asked her who the father was she answered, "I'm not sure...there was more than one." My world went black.

Unbeknownst to me, her own mother, Chloe had adopted a very promiscuous lifestyle. This was a side of our daughter that we were totally unaware of until now.

The doctors convened and then called us into their office. We sat huddled together, sobbing. "I'm sorry, Mom," Chloe moaned repeatedly.

Have I been such a bad mother? Have I failed my daughter? I wondered. *Was Chloe hurting so much that her insecurity caused her to sin?* There were no obvious answers. My guilt was overwhelming, but my sorrow was even more devastating. I felt no anger, just an aching disappointment. Visions of my daughter's life flashed before me. Jim sat in silence, trying to comfort us.

"I can make a call, and we can take care of this right away," our doctor suggested.

The three of us were stunned by his words. "I'm not having an abortion!" Chloe cried. "I won't."

The doctor continued, "Chloe, you are too young to have this child, and it's the best thing for everyone concerned."

"But we're Christians," I muttered. At that very moment Satan whispered in my ear, *If you were such good Christians your daughter wouldn't be pregnant.*

The doctor briefly mentioned adoption as an option, then began making a case for abortion. Have you ever been in a place where you were tempted, even while what was being presented to you went against everything you believed? What the doctor said was making sense. If we chose his way, everything would be over in a few days, and no one would ever know.

Even Chloe and Jim were being swayed by the doctor's suggestions. *Lord,* I prayed, *You promise in Your Word that You will not allow us to be tempted beyond what we can bear. Lord, pull us all out of the mire.* I knew that, although the doctor could end the pregnancy, the sin would bring about tremendous pain for all of us.

We rode home silently, each of us weighing the options. With Chloe and Jim's support, I arranged for an appointment at an adoption agency. The next day the three of us sat listening to the adoption procedures. Then we prayed together and found ourselves in complete agreement: We would put our trust in God and reject the doctor's suggestion to abort.

The next few months were difficult. I confess that when my daughter had problems with her pregnancy, I hoped that God would take the baby so we wouldn't have to continue walking this painful path. *Lord,* I prayed, *wouldn't this be better for everyone concerned?* I struggled daily with my feelings, but I continued trusting God, knowing that He was omniscient. Whatever the outcome, He knew what He was doing.

During my daughter's pregnancy, I was deeply hurt by the gossip of our "friends" and fellow church members. It didn't seem fair that we had chosen the path of obedience and were being crucified for it. Daily I searched the Scriptures. God comforted me with words He had originally given to the Israelites: "Do not be afraid; you will not suffer shame. Do not fear disgrace; you will not be humiliated" (Isaiah 54:4). I continued to believe that our future would be brighter than our present.

Chloe delivered a healthy, seven-pound baby girl, whom she immediately gave to the adoptive parents she had chosen. The three of them had decided that an open adoption would be best for the baby. In an open adoption, the mother stays in contact with the child through photographs and letters and is even given opportunities to visit the family. The thought horrified me; I wanted Chloe to put all this behind her. But it was her decision to make.

My granddaughter is now eight years old. The child who I once wished didn't exist has become the light of my life. To Chloe, who is now grown, she's more like a niece than a daughter—but she has no anxiety about the adoptive family or the quality of upbringing. The adoptive parents are like members of our own family, although we are very conscious of their need for privacy.

Seeking God first brought blessing beyond belief into our lives. I received confirmation of this through my daughter's friend Jessica, who visited Chloe while she was in the hospital. At the time, Jessica had just been released from a hospital for treatment of an eating disorder. When she visited my daughter, she said, "Chloe, I'm so glad you didn't have an abortion. Every girl I met while in the treatment center who has had an abortion suffers so much guilt. You made the right decision."

Truly, the outcome of our situation was nothing short of a miracle. God provided all that we hoped for and more as we leaned on Him and sought His wisdom. I am so thankful.

Emma is living proof that should you be buffeted by this storm, God will never leave you. He is our ever-present help: steady through storms, hope-giving through hurricanes, and redeeming through rain. He is always present, full of love and forgiveness. Run to His shelter.

> *To bring up a child in the way he should go,*
> *travel that way yourself once in a while.*
> JOSH BILLINGS

THE DAD WHO NEVER GAVE UP

I would like to offer a fresh perspective through the eyes of a child. When Kimberly Shumate was a rebellious teen, her father stood on God's promises—and this stand affected his daughter for life. I will let Kimberly tell her story.

I can sum up a troubled kid's world in a word: misery. My mother died when I was seventeen years old. So great was my father's loss that he mourned day and night. I could hardly stand to be at home after she passed away. So I dropped out of school and found a new home on the streets of the city where I lived. My new friends (better known as mall rats) taught me the art of self-preservation. I learned how to lie, steal, defend myself, and disengage from society.

Was I relieved to be out of the house of mourning? Did my new lifestyle satisfy me? Hardly. My life had suddenly gone dark; as I fumbled for the light switch, I sank into depression. What's a kid to do when all seems lost? The answer: toughen up! I worked to harden myself to the world and everyone in it. I took refuge in my emotional deep freeze. It's easier not to feel anything than to feel everything. As time passed I grew colder, continued to disregard my conscience, and became numb to my emotions.

My mall friends saw promise in me. They accepted me for who I was and offered an exciting new agenda. We smoked pot, drank, and spent our time loitering in pool halls and dance clubs. The heavy makeup on my face did a fair job of hiding the fear I harbored inside. But whether I looked the part or not, I was still a child.

I picked up some new hobbies. Spells, hexes, magic wands, Ouija boards, yoga, levitation, spirit channeling, ESP, crystal gazing, runes, tarot cards, and pendulums became a way of life. As I met others who practiced these activities, I experienced a sense of belonging. This exclusive metaphysical society appealed to the child in me who was eager to be accepted. Once I was involved, I was part of something important. I was different; I was special. And unlike high school sports or clubs, this group required no physical capabilities or leadership aptitude. It was an easy sell. Looking back, I see how easily Satan deceived me into believing that I had been given "the power within." It's an old story—"Take a bite from this apple, Eve, and you will be like God."

Soon I was taking the Greyhound every weekend to a bigger city. Gay discos became my sanctuary, because everyone was free to pretend that they were someone else. The men dressed like women, the women looked like men. I was living out a glamorous fairy tale full of lights, glitter, and fun. It made me forget who I was. I could do anything, be anyone. The best part was that I felt accepted. I loved my new friends, and I was viewing the world through a hypnotic lens.

I began doing stage shows and living with a woman impersonator named Wanda. Life finally seemed to be turning out like I wanted. After enrolling in a twelve-week beauty school course, I earned a manicurist's license and eventually relocated to Atlanta to be closer to my father. Even though I had removed myself from family, I still longed to be close to my dad, who had never stopped expressing concern for me.

At that time, the punk rock subculture was the best excuse to dress and act flamboyantly. I dyed my hair a brilliant shade of purple and pierced my ears five times. I adorned my body with safety pins, powdered my face white, and painted my lips black, because I genuinely enjoyed frightening people. It gave me a sense of power and control. I felt as though the world couldn't touch me, as though no one could hurt me. I pierced my ears three more times, the last with a dull needle—it took about ten minutes for the point to make its way through the cartilage. I took pleasure in the pain—as strange as it sounds, it came as a shock that I could still feel.

Despite my years of experimentation, my dad never gave up on me. I remember when my father took our family to dinner at a fancy restaurant. People stared unabashedly, pointed, and made rude comments. It was the late seventies, and nice girls didn't walk around the city sporting purple hair and wearing stage costumes. But my father, the sweetest of men, took my arm in his and escorted me to our table.

My siblings, too, remained fiercely loyal. Still, their love could not repair the hurt I tried so desperately to disguise.

My father remained my anchor. He saw beneath my harsh exterior, and he never stopped praying for the woman he knew I would one day become. Hebrews 11:1 exemplifies his belief in me: "Faith is the substance of things hoped for, the evidence of things not seen." My father viewed me as a priceless jewel set in the Savior's crown.

Despite my father's love, I continued down the path of exploration. In Atlanta, I met a man who owned a local punk rock club. Along with a group of my party-going friends, off to the club I would go every night. My boyfriend developed cocaine and heroin habits, and he often took the drugs simultaneously. At times his life hung in the balance. Sometimes he would call me to come over. It took exactly twenty minutes to make it to his hotel room. When I arrived, I always found his door wide open and him lying unconscious on the bed. For a while we lived together in a warehouse in a dangerous part of the city. He would lock me in from the outside when he left for work at night. I would lie in bed and listen to vagrants climb up the sides of the building and race along the roofline, trying to break in.

My dad continued to pray for me. He adhered to the belief that I would one day come to my senses—and to the Savior. And do you know what? He was right. It took years, but I eventually sickened of my lifestyle. My journey finally led me to the Cross, and there I surrendered.

When a person mired in depression and self-loathing comes to know Christ's forgiveness, the experience is overwhelming. I could hardly contain my gratitude. It's like the parable of the two men who both carried debt: One owed much more than the other, and when both debts were canceled, the one who had owed more was the most grateful. So it was with me.

I couldn't wait to tell my dad—I knew that he would be thrilled. Sure enough, he was overjoyed to hear, "Dad, I've been born again!"

Strangely enough, that was the day when my siblings actually began to look at me funny. My brother and sisters couldn't believe it when I gave up smoking, cursing, fighting, and living with my boyfriend. They watched as a smile replaced my despair.

I had a joy in my heart that I had never known before. And to think that it took only twenty-nine years of praying! I am so thankful that my dad didn't give up on me. Instead, he gave me the most valuable of gifts: He stood in the gap.

I've decided that it doesn't matter how long the trip takes, so long as you eventually get there. I now work for a Christian publishing company in my hometown and am so blessed to be there. The Word speaks truth when it says that love never fails. The devil held me hostage for many, many years, but God's plan for my life was sovereign. He waited for just the right time and just the right place to lead me from darkness into light.

Kimberly's story underscores the effect a praying parent can have, even in the most destitute situation. Take courage. We have a Friend who hears our cries in the storm.

We cannot destroy kindred: Our chains stretch a little sometimes,
but they never break.
MARIE DE RABUTIN-CHANTAL

PROMISES TO STAND ON

Promise: "Some trust in chariots and some in horses, but we trust in the name of the LORD our God. They are brought to their knees and fall, but we rise up and stand firm" (Psalm 20:7–8).

The difference between those who are crushed by storms and those who stand in them is their faith. The wise parent realizes that she cannot by her own power create healthy, happy children. She knows that she can give parenting her best effort, but that God, the author of all good things, is the only one who can recover, restore, and renew wayward children. The wise mother rises up and stands firm in her faith before the heavenly Father. She trusts Him to accomplish all that she cannot.

While you are waiting for your child to find his way back home, what can you do?

- Stand on the promises.
- Pray for your child's salvation, his protection, his mate, his decisions, his friends, and his acceptance of God's plan for his life.
- Praise your child for all the positive things in his life.
- Do not accept or condone behavior that is not biblical.
- Love your child unconditionally. Hate the sin, but love the sinner.
- Focus on his salvation and not on his lifestyle.
- Accept God's plan for your child's life and trust in Him. Remember that each child belongs to God, not to you. Allow your child to be the person God intends for him to be, not the person you want him to be.
- Avoid criticism.
- Compliment your child at least once a day.
- Do all that you can to help your child fulfill his dreams.
- Forgive your child as you yourself have been forgiven (Ephesians 4:31). In turn, seek your child's forgiveness when you have wronged him.

I am like a little pencil in God's hand. He does the writing.
The pencil has nothing to do with it.

MOTHER TERESA

Promise: "Great is our LORD, and mighty in power; his understanding has no limit. The LORD sustains the humble but casts the wicked to the ground" (Psalm 147:5–6).

Only God can sustain us through the heartbreaking storm of a child's rebellion. Let us look to Him for the strength to do that. Let us turn to His unfailing light.

I would like to share a devotional that has moved me to faith time and again. I think every parent should obtain a copy of this and read it often. It reminds me not to interfere in God's plan for my daughter's life, not to assume that I know more than He does. In my desire to help Meg, I have often longed to make her life easier, to cut short the lessons and bring on the relief. But in the effort to make life less difficult for our children, we sometimes cripple them. We take away the experiences that might serve to strengthen and mold them. We need to keep our hands to ourselves and our prayers rising heavenward!

For nearly a year I kept the flask-shaped cocoon of an emperor moth. It is very peculiar in construction. A narrow opening is left in the neck of the flask, through which the mature insect forces its way. This leaves the forsaken cocoon as untouched as one still tenanted, with no rupture of the interlacing fibers. The great disproportion between the means of egress and the size of the imprisoned insect makes one wonder how the exit is accomplished—it is never without great difficulty. The pressure to which the moth's body is subjected in passing through such a narrow opening is a provision of nature to force the juices into the vessels of the wings, these being less developed at the period of emergence from the chrysalis than in other insects.

I was present to witness my imprisoned moth's first effort to escape its confinement. From time to time throughout a forenoon, I watched it patiently struggle to get out. It never seemed to get beyond a certain point, however, and at last my patience was exhausted. *Probably the confining fibers are drier and less elastic than if the cocoon had been left all winter on its native heather, as nature meant it to be,* I thought. In any event, I thought myself wiser than its Maker, and I resolved to give the moth a helping hand. With the point of my scissors I snipped the confining threads, making the exit just a little wider. Immediately, with perfect ease, my moth crawled out. It had shriveled wings, and was dragging a grossly swollen body.

I waited to see the marvelous process of expansion develop before my eyes; as I traced the wings' exquisite markings, all there in miniature, I longed to watch them assume their due proportions and for the creature to emerge, in all its splendor, as one of the loveliest of its kind. But I waited in vain. My false tenderness had proved the moth's ruin. It never came to anything but a stunted creature, crawling painfully through a brief life which it should have spent soaring through the air on rainbow wings.

I have thought of my moth often when I watch with pitying eyes those who struggle with sorrow, suffering, and distress; and I would fain cut short the discipline and give deliverance. Shortsighted man! How knew I that one of these pangs or groans should be spared? The farsighted, perfect love that seeks the perfection of its object does not weakly shrink from present, transient suffering. Our Father's love is too true to be weak. Because He loves His children, He chastises them that they may be partakers of His holiness. With this glorious end in view, He spares not for their crying. Made perfect through sufferings, as the elder brother was, the sons of God are trained up to obedience and brought to glory through much tribulation.[1]

At every step the child should be allowed to meet the real experiences of life; the thorns should never be plucked from his roses.

ELLEN KEY

CONCLUSION: GET OUT OF THE WIND

This storm may seem eternal, but isn't motherhood? No one automatically stops being a mother when her child turns eighteen. A mother remains a mother forever. While the storm winds blow, remember that no child can escape God's loving embrace. He is watching; He is keeping track; He is feeling the most profound parental concern for your child. And He already knows what will be the result of your faithful prayers.

A friend of mine's son chose to live a destructive lifestyle during his teen years. When he was in his twenties, he experienced an incredible conversion. Today he is a minister. My friend told me that when she sits in his congregation, she still has to pinch herself. It still seems unreal to her. Years of prayer changed her son's life. "I was the widow who kept going before the judge until justice was done [Luke 18:1–8]," she told me, laughing. "Every time I fell to my knees in prayer, I felt that the Lord must be thinking, *Not you again!* I was determined that Satan wasn't going to win, and he didn't."

Even while his parents were unable to influence this young man, God was watching over him. He finally brought him home. Isn't it great to know that what seems hopeless to humans is easy for God?

I will let Kimberly, who told us her victorious story earlier, close this chapter. She encourages other parents to stand in the parental storm, to place their hope in the Lord: "Please, please, never give up on your sons and daughters. Keep standing, keep praying, and keep hoping. I don't care how young or how old your child is, or whether he is a psychic, a rock star, or a murderer sitting behind bars. No one, and I mean no one, is exempt from God's love and mercy."

Amen!

> *The most important thing she'd learned over the years*
> *was that there was no way to be a perfect mother and*
> *a million ways to be a good one.*
>
> JILL CHURCHILL

CHAPTER EIGHT

THE DEATH OF A MARRIAGE

Faith is the only known cure for fear.
LENA K. SADLER

Two things are true of divorce: It happens, and it hurts. No woman who ever stood radiantly before a minister, her beloved at her side, expected the relationship to founder. She never pictured herself arguing across a lawyer's desk, packing her bags, speaking the wrenching words, "It's over." When faced with the unthinkable, she agonizes, *What in the world happened? Where did our love go? Will I ever recover from this nightmare?*

I asked those awful questions. I choked on the disappointment, the disillusionment, and the despair that the end of my marriage generated. I dealt with the legal issues, coped with my child's anguish, and wondered about my own future. I prayed anguished prayers and searched my heart to determine if anything good could ever come my way again. In short, I stood smack in the middle of this devastating storm.

I asked myself the same questions you may be facing: "As my marriage dissolves, how do I keep my knees from buckling beneath the load of guilt? How do I face all the loved ones who believed in me, hoped for me? Most importantly, how do I retain faith in God when He seems to be silent?"

You already know what my answer will be: by standing on the promises of Christ. By believing, against all odds and despite all appearances, that God will empower you to keep the faith, to provide for your family, and to continue standing in the midst of this storm. I believe, because I know God's Word, that your pain will eventually end in rest.

HIS WAY IS BEST—HIS WAY IS REST

Key Promise: "Are you tired? Worn out? Burned out on religion? Come to me. Get away with me and you'll recover your life. I'll show you how to take a real rest. Walk with me and work with me— watch how I do it. Learn the unforced rhythms of grace. I won't lay anything heavy or ill-fitting on you. Keep company with me and you'll learn to live freely and lightly" (Matthew 11:28–30, *The Message*).

Let me begin by saying that in this chapter I will not attempt to know God's clear perspective on divorce. I do, however, believe that both abuse and adultery are biblical grounds for it. Deciding whether or not your situation justifies ending your marriage—and having to admit that sometimes the decision is made for you despite your wishes—is very difficult and best left to you and a trusted Christian counselor. I write today to those women for whom divorce is a reality, for whatever reason, and who wish to learn survival skills to get through this shattering storm.

If you are enduring the biting winds of divorce, you more than likely find yourself relating to the psalmist's words—"O Lord, have mercy on me in my anguish. My eyes are red from weeping; my health is broken from sorrow. I am pining away with grief; my years are shortened, drained away because of my sadness.... I stoop with sorrow and with shame" (Psalm 31:9–10, TLB). Do you taste nothing but tears, see nothing but darkness, feel nothing but loneliness?

Friend, I have stood in your shoes. Take my hand, and we'll find a better place to stand. In these hours when you feel as though you're living in a daze, you need some sure footing, and God's Word offers it. As the psalmist cried out, "I was trusting you, O Lord. I said, 'You alone are my God; my times are in your hands. Rescue me from those who hunt me down relentlessly. Let your favor shine again upon your servant; save me just because you are so kind!'" (Psalm 31:14–16, TLB)

First, remember that He is our God and that we belong to Him. "Long before he laid down earth's foundations, he had us in mind, had settled on us as the focus of his love, to be made whole and holy by his love. Long, long ago he decided to adopt us into his family through Jesus Christ" (Ephesians 1:4–5, *The Message*). Even the loneliest is not alone. Anyone who has the Lord has close kin—*family*—to help get through the ordeal of divorce.

Second, know that your life is in His hands. Every moment passes only because He allows it. "The eternal God is your refuge, and underneath are the everlasting arms" (Deuteronomy 33:27). His knowledge is perfect, and His faithfulness is everlasting.

Third, acknowledge that God is kind. He is not wishy-washy; His character is abiding, and His love does not change. "Jehovah is kind and merciful, slow to get angry, full of love. He is good to everyone, and his compassion is intertwined with everything he does.... The Lord lifts the fallen and those bent beneath their loads.... The Lord is fair in everything he does, and full of kindness. He is close to all who call on him sincerely" (Psalm 145:8–9, 14, 17–18, TLB).

Anyone who has fought the battle of depression and despair following a divorce can testify that God is faithful and true. He is working out His plan even today. Though you may not be able to see the plan, it is in motion. You have this reassurance from God: "It's in Christ that we find out who we are and what we are living for. Long before he first heard of Christ and got our hopes up, he had his eye on us, had designs on us for glorious living, part of the overall purpose he is working out in everything and everyone" (Ephesians 1:11–12, *The Message*).

As you stumble across the bridge to where God wants you—in glorious living—listen to these stories from other storm survivors. Keep walking toward His rest. Know that our kind God is with you, waiting to reveal a freer and lighter way of life, and hang on.

My life is…a mystery which I do not attempt to really understand,
as though I were led by the hand in a night
where I see nothing, but can fully depend on the love
and protection of Him who guides me.

THOMAS MERTON

MY OWN STORY: STORM CLOUDS BREWING…

There are signs that a spouse is having an affair. Suddenly he begins paying extra attention to his appearance. He may work out more often. There are unexplained absences—a simple trip to the store might last for hours. He loses interest in his family and begins working longer hours at the office. Sometimes the old, clichéd signs give him away—lipstick on his collar, strange perfume on his clothes, his buddies' sympathetic glances toward his wife.

The signs are always there, but often the spouse refuses to acknowledge them. She doesn't really want to know; perhaps if she ignores them they will go away.

I discovered that my marriage was over some time after it had ended: One night when my husband wasn't home at midnight, I went to bed. After watering my pillow with my tears, I fell asleep begging God to reveal what I should do.

At two o'clock in the morning, I awoke suddenly. I felt the Lord clearly instructing me to get up. *But Lord, where will I go?* I wondered. I tried to ignore the command, but the Lord's urging was too strong.

I rose from bed, dressed, loaded my sleeping child into the car, and began driving.

I didn't need to go far. At the end of my street I found my husband in a car with another woman. I didn't stop driving; I didn't slow down. I simply turned the car around and drove home. Then I climbed back into bed and waited.

When my husband came home, he undressed in silence and went to sleep without explanation. And in the days that followed, he let me know that he no longer wanted to be married to me.

In the weeks that followed, I prayed for a miracle. I sought counseling from wise and godly people. I pleaded with my husband. I went to the church library and read every book I could find on how to save a marriage. Christian men and women who had found victory over adultery shared their testimonies with us. Our minister encouraged us to put it all behind.

I finally did that. I forgave my husband, hoping it would prove the key to our future together. But his mind was made up. As far as he was concerned, our marriage was over.

In the south we have an old saying: "When life gets to be too much, a lady takes to her bed." That's exactly what I did. I pulled the covers over my head, hoping and praying that it was all a bad dream from which I would soon wake up. I cried buckets of tears. But God seemed fresh out of miracles and was oddly silent.

One day my friend Evelyn Inman, who has suffered through many personal tragedies, strapped on her artificial legs (she'd lost both to diabetes), came over to my house, and climbed the long staircase to my bedroom. She gently washed my face with a warm, damp cloth and convinced me that if she could get up from her bed after losing two legs, I could surely get up after losing a deceitful husband.

To my surprise, she was right! I got up and got busy. My husband had not only left his family and his home, but he had also left us in dire financial straits. I went back to work full time, and Evelyn moved in to care for Megan. My friends Jane Kerr and Ann Morris brought us food during those lean days.

Despite the support and help of our loving friends and family, my daughter and I had a lot of recovering to do. Megan struggled daily with her father's absence, and I ached for her. Whenever she and Evelyn weren't looking, I cried uncontrollably, wondering what would become of us. I couldn't understand my heavenly Father's distance at this painful point in my life. Where was He? Why wasn't He helping? Day after day my life felt like it was ending. God was all I had to cling to, so cling I did.

Attending my church at that point just sharpened the pain. I was keenly aware of the empty spot beside me that my husband used to fill. I would sit, watching the happy, whole families, and remember better days. Would I ever be happy—or whole—again? I felt worse after every service.

One Sunday I drove to a new church. The minister, Dr. Paul Walker, was a man whom I had heard years before at an awards ceremony. He had so impressed me that I had found out where he pastored. That Sunday I felt like I was reaching for a lifeline from heaven. Maybe this man would provide the healing words I needed.

When he stepped to the pulpit, I immediately felt comforted. As he began to pray, I drank in every word. Then, unexpectedly, he prayed, "There is someone here today whose husband has left her; God wants her to know that everything is going to be all right. He has a very special plan for her life!" His words echoed throughout the sanctuary. I lifted my head and looked around—at least three thousand people were attending this service. Did God intend this message for me, or was it for one of the many other women sitting alone? *Surely he isn't referring to me,* I thought in panic.

The minister then repeated the words. It was as though God were trying to tell me, *Yes, you, Susan!* I accepted them and left church that day with my head high and a skip in my step. I knew now that everything would really be all right. The wonderful promise from God rang in my mind, "'I know the plans I have for you,' declares the LORD, 'plans to prosper you and not to harm you, plans to give you hope and a future'" (Jeremiah 29:11).

Did the pain dissolve? Did I embrace a new life and live happily ever after? Hardly. I still wept. I still experienced intense feelings of loneliness and rejection. I still wrestled with God in prayer. But what kept me going was the knowledge that God had a plan, and that all this torment would eventually amount to something.

For a time, I continued to live in hope that my husband would see the light and return home. I asked a trusted friend to pray and fast with me about this. For three days we sought the Lord together. At the end of our fast, I still didn't know if my husband would ever come back, but I did have a new assurance that God was going to take care of Meg and me.

I previously revealed some of the ways in which God provided for Meg and me in the years following, so I won't repeat them here. As it turned out, God was never out of miracles. He was pouring them upon me all the time—through my friends and family, through work, through every step I took. The point I want to make is that recovery begins with faith in God's ability to make any situation, even divorce, beautiful and whole and life giving. Elisabeth Elliot, who has twice tasted the grief of widowhood, sums up this truth beautifully:

> When we were very small our parents taught us to trust Him; they sang to us at bedtime, "Safe in the Arms of Jesus." That's where we grew up.
>
> But safety, as the Cross shows, does not exclude suffering. All that was of course beyond me when I was a child, but as I began to learn about suffering I learned that *trust* in

those strong arms means that even our suffering is under control. We are not doomed to meaninglessness. A loving Purpose is behind it all, a great tenderness even in the fierceness.[1]

Friend, reach out for that tenderness. He is near.

> *God is our clothing, that wraps, clasps and*
> *encloses us so as to never leave us.*
> JULIAN OF NORWICH

FALLING BLOWS, FALTERING DREAMS

Annie and Eddie seemed like the happiest couple ever. Their courtship and subsequent wedding were the stuff of which fairy tales are made. The attractive lovebirds both came from Christian families, were active in their church, looked forward to promising careers, and had many similar interests. Everyone thought that their relationship possessed all the ingredients for a successful marriage.

But appearances never tell the whole story. I will let Annie relate what happened.

Following the reception, Eddie's parents hosted a party for the out-of-town guests. As the night wore on, I began to feel the effects of a long, albeit wonderful, day. Eagerly anticipating the honeymoon, I whispered playfully to my groom, "Let's go."

Eddie's face took on a strange expression, one that I had never before seen. Rage shone in his eyes as he said fiercely, "We'll go when I'm ready." His words were spoken loudly, obviously intended to impress the guests.

I shrank back, puzzled. *He must be showing off,* I realized. *I should just leave him alone.*

Much later, after most of the guests had departed, I tried again. "Ed, I'm so tired. Can we please go?"

Again he became furious—but at least we left. Ed spun the tires in the driveway and began tearing down the street toward our hotel. I had known that he possessed somewhat of a temper, but it had never been directed at me. Not once during our dating days had he gotten angry at me. There in the car, I began to tremble.

After a few blocks Eddie turned and shouted at me, "I'll teach you to tell me what to do in front of people!" The car swerved toward the curb. Eddie pulled onto a side road and slammed on the brakes. He grabbed a handful of my hair and yelled, "Just because I married you doesn't mean you are going to tell me what to do!"

Terrified, I looked into his eyes—the very eyes I had thought I knew so well—and saw no love, only anger. "I'm sorry," I sobbed. I begged him to release me as tears slid down my face.

"Don't ever let it happen again," he warned.

I tried to explain—"I was tired—" but Eddie grabbed my hair again and smashed my face into the dashboard.

I can't tell you the horror that I felt then. My head throbbed and my mind was reeling. Eddie and I had dated for three years; his short fuse had never been at issue. I had not even suspected the depth of his anger, let alone that I might be its eventual target. I was stunned and confused.

Should I leave him? What will everyone say if I leave him on our wedding night? I looked down at the linen suit I was wearing. I felt as crumpled as it looked.

Suddenly I felt like I was coming out of a daze. I opened the car door and began running down the dark road. There was no way I would stay married to an abusive man—no way! I ran faster. If Ed behaved this way on our honeymoon, how would he treat me after we had been married for several years? I wasn't going to stick around to find out.

Ed started following me in the car. He pulled up next to me and rolled down the car window. "I'm sorry, Annie," he said. "It was the pressure of the wedding. It will never happen again. Please get in."

I slowed to a walk, but I didn't respond.

"Come on," he pleaded. "Let's go enjoy our honeymoon."

"No," I told him. I wouldn't look at him.

"Annie, please, you know how much I love you. Get in."

I hesitated. After a few minutes he had me worn down. I worried about how I might explain divorce to my family and friends. I thought they would say that I had lost my mind, that I had been unfair in not giving Ed another chance.

Reluctantly, I got back into the car. We drove to the hotel to celebrate our honeymoon, as best we could under the circumstances.

I wish that I had never gotten back into the car. That night unleashed a cycle of abuse that I was eventually powerless to stop. Every time Ed lost his temper and struck me, I left him. Then he would apologize profusely, and I would relent. Every time I returned, the beatings grew worse.

I reached a point at which I felt obligated not only to forgive him, but to return to him. I told myself that Ed was a sick man and that I had vowed to stand by him in sickness and in health. I now know that God neither expects nor desires for us to remain in abusive relationships. I wanted my marriage to work so desperately that I refused to admit defeat. I repeatedly put my life in danger for fear of disappointing anyone—including myself.

My marriage finally ended—not when I refused to submit to any more beatings, but when Eddie left me for another woman. And with him went my dream of a happy marriage.

Annie had gotten so caught up in the cycle of abuse that she lost part of herself. What happened to the strong, outgoing, successful woman she had once been? Frightened, insecure, and withdrawn, Annie attempted to hide her shame by distancing herself from family and friends. Annie didn't understand that God's command to forgive the person who harms her does not require her to remain in the relationship. Forgiveness can take place without reunion.

After her husband left, Annie was devastated over the loss of both the marriage and the dream she had for marriage. She had done everything possible to protect her husband should he eventually come to his senses. In keeping the abuse a secret, she cut herself off from anyone who could have helped her. Frightened and alone, Annie finally turned to the church. It was there that she received healing.

Annie leans on Jesus' promise: "The thief comes only to steal and kill and destroy; I have come that they may have life, and have it to the full" (John 10:10). She found restoration through the love and compassion of Christian friends and, ultimately, through Jesus Christ.

Today she says, "I have not remarried, but God has blessed me with a full life. If I ever marry again, I will choose a husband who loves me just as Christ loves the church: 'Husbands ought to love their wives as their own bodies. He who loves his wife loves himself. After all, no one ever hated his own body, but he feeds and cares for it, just as Christ does the church—for we are members of his body' (Ephesians 5:28–30). Eddie obviously had no love for himself," she continues. "Feeling unlovable after the abusive marriage, I found myself worthy of love through Jesus Christ my Lord."

Annie experienced some of the hardest lessons that life can teach, but she has survived them. She now knows what "life to the full" is all about!

> *…What really broke a heart was taking away its dream—*
> *whatever the dream might be.*
>
> PEARL S. BUCK

LIFE LESSONS

My dear friend Gilda dreamed of becoming the wife of a successful husband and of one day raising a family. When she married her high school sweetheart, Johnny, Gilda believed that they would have a wonderful life together and that she would fulfill all of her hopes for the future. Although Johnny was not a believer like her, Gilda felt certain that love would conquer all.

After the wedding, the couple moved to Gastonia, North Carolina, where Johnny attended a junior college. Then they moved to Atlanta, so he could complete his degree in engineering. Still deeply committed to her dream, Gilda dropped out of college and worked full time to support her husband while he was in college. When Gilda's best friend Renee visited Atlanta to help them settle into their new apartment, Renee decided to relocate there herself. Gilda was thrilled to have her hometown friend as her neighbor.

Gilda was shocked to discover the affair. The evenings that Johnny had told her he was studying at the library, he had actually been spending with Renee.

Though she felt betrayed, Gilda was willing to forgive and eager to put her marriage back together. But in counseling, Johnny told her flatly that he had no interest in changing things and no intention of mending his ways.

Following the divorce, Gilda went to counseling and was able to forgive her ex-husband and her ex-friend. She got her life together and determined to follow the Lord wholeheartedly. Gilda had learned from her mistakes; she now took seriously the Scripture that she had previously ignored, "Do not be yoked together with unbelievers. For what do righteousness and wickedness have in common? Or what fellowship can light have with darkness?" (2 Corinthians 6:14).

When an attractive young attorney named Lee asked Gilda out, she agreed. But when Lee began to pursue her steadily, Gilda told him that she could never consider a serious relationship if he didn't attend church with her. "I have nothing against church," Lee protested. "I believe in God; I just don't go to church. But I'm perfectly willing to go with you."

Lee visited Gilda's church that Sunday and fell in love with everything about it. On the drive home, Gilda was amused to discover that Lee had signed up to serve on the cleanup committee after his first visit. Lee became a committed believer, and Gilda was astonished and thrilled when he grew even more active in the church than she.

Lee and Gilda fell in love and were later married. Without hesitation, they invited God to be at the center of their marriage. They have raised three beautiful children, all of whom were baptized in the church. Their marriage has become a model for many other couples.

Today both Gilda and Lee are leaders in their church, as well as in their community. Lee was elected to city council and is admired for his integrity, ethics, and strong principles. He gives Gilda much of the credit for his success.

With God's help, Gilda's dream of a happy marriage has come true and flourished for over twenty years: "When people ask us about the secret of our happy marriage, we reply, 'Our commitment to God and the church.'" The Morrises have found that their faith in God is the bond that holds their marriage together. "The best is yet to come," Gilda and Lee agree.

Their story proves God's faithfulness to the devastated and His mercy for those who follow His Word: "He heals the brokenhearted and binds up their wounds" (Psalm 147:3).

*Other men see only a hopeless end, but
the Christian rejoices in an endless hope.*

GILBERT M. BEEKEN

PROMISES TO STAND ON

Promise: In Jesus we have a never-ending source of life and hope. "I am the bread of life. No one who comes to me will ever be hungry again. Those who believe in me will never thirst" (John 6:35, NLT).

Maybe *life* and *hope* sound like foreign terms to you today. Maybe you suspect that God's goodness extends to everyone but you. Perhaps lingering pain over mistakes made in your marriage—and we *all* make them—makes you feel estranged from His promises, separated from His supply.

It isn't true. If you feel a wall between yourself and God, you need to begin tearing it down. If you made mistakes, confess them. If you feel guilt, admit it to the Lord. If you feel hopeless, ask Him for hope. And if God still seems distant, seek Him through a friend: Visit a Christian counselor or consult your pastor.

Read biblically sound books. Listen to uplifting music. Pray even when you feel as though the words are left unheard. Keep your heart open and your eyes peeled: He promises to draw near to the one who draws near to Him (James 4:8). Let your hunger for life and hope pull you toward your Savior, not away from him. "The LORD is with you when you are with him. If you seek him, he will be found by you" (2 Chronicles 15:2). He longs to fill you with comfort, with assurance that even now He is repairing the pieces of your life. He specializes in feeding the hungry and refreshing the thirsty. Friend, seek Him, and you will be found by Him.

How can God direct our steps if we're not taking any?
SARAH LEAH GRAFSTEIN

Promise: "'Do not be afraid; you will not suffer shame. Do not fear disgrace; you will not be humiliated. You will forget the shame of your youth and remember no more the reproach of your widowhood. For your Maker is your husband—the LORD Almighty is his name—the Holy One of Israel is your Redeemer; he is called the God of all the earth. The LORD will call you back as if you were a wife deserted and distressed in spirit—a wife who married young, only to be rejected,' says your God" (Isaiah 54:4–6).

- Begin to see God as your husband—your protector, friend, companion, and the love of your life.
- Treat Him as King; seek Him prayerfully in all your decisions.
- Trust Him as Provider; trust Him to meet all your needs.
- Draw near to Him. Make a date to spend regular time alone with Him in prayer, both speaking and listening.
- Embrace His way of life; take up His yoke and give Him your burdens.
- Seek Him in others; spend time in fellowship with other believers to gain knowledge and understanding.
- Stay in His Word; stand on His promises.

God is enough! All religion is enfolded for me now in these three words.
HANNAH WHITALL SMITH

CONCLUSION: RAIN CAN'T DROWN YOU—UNLESS YOU LIE DOWN IN IT!

The force of a storm is only the combination of its far less powerful parts. Wind may be destructive, but outside of a storm's wild pushes it is often gentle. Driving rain may be blinding, but rain showers are actually quite refreshing. And clouds by themselves are lovely: billowy, soft, dreamy looking. Only when combined with pressure and precipitation do they turn dark and menacing. A storm really is only the sum of its parts. And experienced one at a time, each is not all that threatening.

So it is with the storm of divorce. Take each phase one step at a time. The enforced separation from your mate, the changes in your lifestyle, the finances, the children, the new daily routine, the altered holiday gatherings—don't try to resolve all these issues at once. They will overwhelm you. Take them on one at a time, and they will seem infinitely less foreboding.

My friend Margaret endured a stormy divorce when she was in her seventies, and her calm attitude throughout spoke volumes about her faith. She was left with almost no money, though her ex-husband was a millionaire. Those of us who loved Margaret suggested she consult a lawyer—surely something could be done. But the attorney assured Margaret that her settlement was set in stone. He recommended that she visit a financial planner so she could learn to live on her meager income.

When Margaret told me the story, I was furious. I cried to the Lord, *It's so unfair!* How could her ex-husband live like a king while this godly woman struggled to make ends meet? It wasn't as though she could just go out and get a job. I said this to Margaret, who replied sweetly, "God has a better plan."

"I can't imagine what that might be," I muttered bitterly. (As you can see, I don't always stand on God's promises for my friends!)

"He's never once let me down in over seventy years," Margaret reminded me. "He's not going to let me down now."

I was sobbing as I hung up the phone. Sulkily, I prayed that God would indeed meet my friend's needs.

A few months later I received a phone call. When I answered, I heard the same sweet voice say, "This is Margaret. I'm calling to tell you about God's better plan." She shared how her neighbor, the wife of an elderly doctor, had died.

As time passed, however, the good doctor invited Margaret to ride with him to church one morning. A few Sunday drives led to a dinner invitation. And over dinner one night, the widower confessed that he was in love with Margaret. The two were married soon thereafter, and Margaret has never had to worry about finances since!

What a wonderful lesson. God *always* has a better plan than we can imagine if we will only give Him time to put it together. As you make your way through this storm, let God's plan care for your every worry.

> *God's best gifts put man's best dreams to shame.*
> ELIZABETH BARRETT BROWNING

CHAPTER NINE

THE ULTIMATE SORROW

Mourning is not forgetting. It is an undoing.
Every minute tie has to be untied and something permanent
and valuable recovered and assimilated from the knot.

MARGERY ALLINGHAM

*I*t has been called the "amputation without anesthesia."
Some react to its occurrence by turning to stone—saying
little, living less. Others dissolve in bouts of emotion too
overpowering to fight. And some reach deep inside for a filament of
will and discover unexpected springs through which to again love
and hope and laugh.

The catalyst for these scenarios is the death of a loved one.
Though long illnesses provide some preparation for the coming loss,
it is impossible to build up a buffer that will completely cover you
during this stinging storm. As long as you continue to love, you will
hurt when your beloved is taken.

At some point, you have probably witnessed the devastating
effect of grief, either your own or someone else's. In extreme cases
you may have wondered if survival were possible—even preferable.
Some of you may have watched loved ones collapse beneath the
pain and never quite recover; others—to your surprise and possibly
their own—find themselves still standing and embracing life after
loss.

How do survivors pull it off? How can you endure the gale-force winds and searing lightning strikes that grief brings? How can you transform emotional paralysis into acceptance and peace? How can you justify living when the center of your earthly love leaves you? Friend, you can do all this and immeasurably more when you turn to the Healer of the soul and allow Him to restore what death and shock have stolen. When you send your roots deep into the foundation of God's promises, you stop trying to float along on feeling. Over time, sense replaces sensibility and your soul is strengthened. God is able, *especially* when you are not. (Read that last sentence again.)

EVEN IN THIS DARKEST PLACE, GOD'S LIGHT WILL NOT FAIL YOU

Key Promise: "Do not fear, for I am with you; Do not anxiously look about you, for I am your God. I will strengthen you, surely I will help you. Surely I will uphold you with My righteous right hand" (Isaiah 41:10, NASB).

This is a storm that no one escapes. Sooner or later, death steals away someone you know and love. I experienced the death of a friend for the first time as a teenager. My friend Jimmy was a very popular athlete. Everyone in our school adored him. I had been his date to the annual football banquet, a very important event. Jimmy had a crush on me, but I didn't return his romantic affection—in fact, on the last day I saw him, I had just turned down a date with him. He drove away, never to return. He was only sixteen years old when he was killed in a car accident that day.

A few days later my friends and I sat weeping beside his casket in a funeral home. His mother was inconsolable. If our grief as his friends was devastating, how deeply felt must have been the pain of the woman who loved him from conception. In seeing death up close for the first time, I thought there could be nothing worse.

As a child, I believed that you died when you were old; by then, all your friends were gone, and you were ready to go, too—right?

And I thought that people always died gracefully—not suddenly. Life wasn't supposed to snatch you away when you were young and vibrant, with your whole life stretched out before you. But in Jimmy's case, it had. Life suddenly didn't seem fair. I wanted so much to make sense of it all.

We asked our parents the *why* questions, but they didn't have the answers. "You have to trust God," they said. "It was His will for Jimmy to die." How could we tell them how difficult it was to trust in the God who had taken our friend away? It seemed too sinful to suggest. Our minister kept assuring us that we would see Jimmy again in heaven one day. Although this was a comforting thought, it didn't completely satisfy. What about now? What about the presence we would miss every day until eternity? I felt as though God were nowhere to be found.

For the first time in my life, my faith wavered. I knew I was at a crossroads: I could reject this seemingly cruel God, or I could take these burning questions to His Word and see what He had to say. I wasn't sure how He would feel about my anger, but I wasn't ready to give up on Him. I was confused, vulnerable, and frightened, but I was determined to know my heavenly Father intimately. I never wanted to experience this degree of isolation again. Surprisingly, this tragedy brought me closer to God and proved a turning point in my life and my faith.

As those of you who have grieved know, the emotions and the questions grief ignites are powerful. I learned during that traumatic period we should never be afraid that our crises are too demanding for truth to conquer. To put it somewhat informally, God is not a wimp! And neither is His Word. He invites us to ask for His help during tragedy, even through the horrors of grief.

The night of my friend's funeral I told my parents good night and took my Bible to bed with me. Flipping through the pages, I came upon the Scripture, "My soul melts from heaviness; strengthen me according to Your word" (Psalm 119:28, NKJV). At that moment, I felt that the Lord both understood me and had given me these words to pray. I suddenly felt certain that I would find the answers to my questions in His Word. It was there I could obtain the strength I needed, the clarity that would empower my faith. So I began to dig.

One Scripture afforded me great comfort and became the foundation of my faith during those confusing days. I found it while reading an account of Jesus' response to the loss of a loved one. In Matthew 14, Herod made a promise to grant his mistress any request. She wanted the head of John the Baptist, who had openly criticized their sinful relationship. Herod arranged for John's beheading and presented the grisly gift to his girlfriend. John's disciples buried his body, then went to tell Jesus.

How did Jesus respond? "When Jesus heard what had happened, he withdrew by boat privately to a solitary place" (Matthew 14:13). While we don't know what Jesus did in those dark hours, I think we can assume that he experienced the human pangs of loss. John the Baptist was both a colleague and a relative, a rare mix of faith and courage. Probably he was a comfort to Jesus, who also bore the burden of a unique and difficult mission. I believe Jesus grieved in that lonely location by Himself. And because of that, I believe He understood my pain when my friend died. Jesus knew what I was feeling.

I was overwhelmed anew by a revelation: God loved us so much that He sent His Son, Jesus Christ, not only to die for our sins, but also to walk on this earth, experiencing all of the beautiful and horrific emotions that life offers the human race. What a gift—a Savior who redeems souls *and* empathizes with our earthly pains! Who better to understand what we are going through than Jesus? He suffered just as we suffer.

The Word confirms this and calls us to come to Jesus for aid:

Now that we know what we have—Jesus, this great High Priest with ready access to God—let's not let it slip through our fingers. We don't have a priest who is out of touch with our reality. He's been through weakness and testing, experienced it all—all but the sin. So let's walk right up to him and get what he is so ready to give. Take the mercy, accept the help. (Hebrews 4:14–16, *The Message*)

Later in the same book, the writer urges us, "Consider him who endured such opposition from sinful men, so that you will not grow weary and lose heart" (Hebrews 12:3).

God does not promise that death will brush us lightly. He recognizes that our human bonds are deep and that loss will wound us, but His promises do offer us the means to survive and even hope again. Let me share some stories of God's faithful illumination in this darkest of storms.

You take a handful of rocks and put them in a jar.
Then once a week, you take one tiny pebble out of the jar and
throw it away. When the jar is empty, why, you'll just about
be over your grief…. Time alone will do if you're short on rocks.
SHARYN MCCRUMB

WAKING FROM A REAL-LIFE NIGHTMARE

My friend Mary has endured the storm of grief. I'll let her tell the story.

When the phone awakened us from a deep sleep, I knew immediately that something was terribly wrong. We listened, shaking, to the news that our son had been in an accident and was at the hospital.

We threw on our clothes and raced to the car, praying all the way to the hospital that Matt would be okay, that the accident wasn't as serious as we feared. Once we reached the hospital, though, we knew the news wasn't good when a nurse ushered us straight into the doctor's office. The physician gently told us that our son had died moments before.

Everything we said and did from that moment I remember through the haze of shock. The doctor led us to Matthew's body so we could say good-bye. Even though we were painfully aware that our son's beautiful spirit was no longer present, we kissed his lips, held his hands, and gently brushed his hair back from his forehead. His body was still warm. I ran my finger over the small scar on his chin. It seemed like yesterday that he had cut himself while shaving for the first time. He was still wearing the madras shirt I had ironed earlier that morning.

If only it was morning again, I thought, *I would hold on to him. I wouldn't let him go to the basketball game after all. I would keep him home. Why can't this just be a bad dream? Why can't I wake up any moment?*

The precious child I had rocked as a baby, the little boy whose skinned knees I had kissed, the teenager I had cheered at ball games—he was gone. My son would never have the opportunity to grow up, marry, establish a career, or raise children. As the truth sank in, my husband and I felt robbed. We grieved not only his presence but also the future joys we would not experience.

In my grief, I was tempted to blame God, but I needed Him too much to turn my back on Him. He sustained me through the dark hours of grief and filled my heart with the hope that I would be reunited in heaven with my son. And He blessed my husband with a supernatural strength: He held me in his arms in the late-night hours as I lay awake wondering why, and he prayed with me. My dear husband laid aside his own grief to minister to me. He carried me down memory lane, and we reminisced about all the happy times we had shared as a family. He told me repeatedly what a good mother I had been to our son and convinced me that I could take comfort in all the joy I had brought into Matt's time on earth.

The body of Christ also held us up in prayer and encouragement. Never have I been so appreciative of our faith.

The biggest question I had to deal with, of course, was why the loving God I served had allowed this hideous thing to happen to Matthew—and to us. Did I ever ask Him? Certainly I did hundreds—no, thousands—of times. And then I stopped. There just was no explanation. After several years I was able to accept what Scripture makes clear, "'My thoughts are completely different from yours,' says the LORD. 'And my ways are far beyond anything you could imagine. For just as the heavens are higher than the earth, so are my ways higher than your ways and my thoughts higher than your thoughts'" (Isaiah 55:8–9, NLT). I realized that I did not have the vision to see the big picture God saw. I wouldn't come to an understanding in this life, so I had to focus on eternity—the day I would see Matt again, as well as finally meet my Savior face-to-face.

I also realized that understanding *why* would not necessarily make Matt's death easier to accept—that the reason didn't really matter. Nothing would alter the fact that one of my children now lived in heaven. What did matter was that my lifelong faith didn't shatter now, when I needed it the most.

I was able to put the whys behind me and face the new day only by relying on God's Word and His promises. Verses about eternity and meeting loved ones there meant everything to me. Slowly, I accepted that Matthew wasn't really gone—just temporarily transferred. I would see him again; my love for him would not be wasted. "He will swallow up death forever. The Sovereign LORD will wipe away the tears" (Isaiah 25:8).

Regarding the question, friends, that has come up about what happens to those already dead and buried, we don't want you in the dark any longer. First off, you must not carry on over them like people who have nothing to look forward to, as if the grave were the last word. Since Jesus died and broke loose from the grave, God will most certainly bring back to life those who died in Jesus.

And then this: We can tell you with complete confidence—we have the Master's word on it—that when the Master comes again to get us, those of us who are still alive will not get a jump on the dead and leave them behind. In actual fact, they'll be ahead of us.... And then there will be one huge family reunion with the Master. So reassure one another with these words (1 Thessalonians 4:13–17, *The Message*).

The thing about grief is that it is never completely finished. Matthew died thirty years ago, and I still feel the ache. As the years passed, I found that while the cutting pain of grief eased, I never stopped missing Matt—his smile, his voice, and his touch. My arms have never stopped longing for my baby. Even though I can name a few positive things that came out of my son's death, I must admit that not one was so positive that it justified losing him.

Even today I feel as if a piece of me is missing. It is simply unnatural for a child to die before his parents do. Mothering manuals never prepare you for this ordeal!

But I can say with certainty that God didn't leave me to face Matthew's death alone. His presence gradually overcame my fear and anger. Where doubt might have sprouted, hope grew. I can't wait to see Matthew again, but I no longer rail at God for taking him. I know he is safely kept until we are together again, and there is real comfort in that: "The righteous pass away; the godly often die before their time.... No one seems to understand that God is protecting them from the evil to come. For the godly who die will rest in peace" (Isaiah 57:1–2, NLT).

Mary's experience, devastating as it was, equipped her to begin a life-changing ministry to other bereaved parents. In a way, Matthew continues to affect the world for good—the love his mother carries for him has blessed many others throughout her lifetime.

> *What we call death was to Him only emigration.*
> AMELIA E. BARR

TIMING IS EVERYTHING!

Another friend describes the pain of losing a brother and the surprising gift God sent to console the family.

My brother Ed was the oldest sibling in my family and gifted in many ways: He was intelligent, handsome, loving, and full of good humor. Everyone adored him. Folks used to say he'd grow up to be president. My sisters and I agreed that he was the greatest big brother in the world.

One New Year's Eve my younger sister Mellie and I climbed into our older sister's featherbed. Janet helped us get covered up. Unbeknownst to Mama and Daddy, the three of us were determined to stay awake to welcome in the New Year. Snuggled beneath layers of quilts, we watched the clock's hands slowly creep toward midnight.

Our anticipation was getting the better of us. We were trying to muffle our giggles under the covers when a series of loud knocks came at the front door. We looked at one another and I asked aloud,

"Who could possibly be knocking on our door at this time of the night?"

"Ed must have come home early from the New Year's Eve celebration," Janet whispered.

"He's going to break down the door if he doesn't stop pounding," Mellie giggled.

Our curiosity became more than we could bear, so we quietly slipped out of bed and tiptoed around the corner. We caught a glimpse of our father pulling on his robe as he hurried toward the door, Mama trailing a few steps behind. Fear and concern clouded their faces as Daddy opened the door. We strained to see who was there.

"It's Uncle John," I told my sisters as we tried to understand the muffled tones. Then we heard a sound coming from my mother, one unlike any I had ever heard: It was the sound of death, a wail from deep within her soul. We raced into the room in time to see Mama collapse in Daddy's arms as Uncle John supported Daddy. In a matter of moments our world had changed forever. Our brother had been killed in a car accident.

The doctor came later that night and sedated Mama; the pain was stealing not only rest but also her ability to function at all. The three of us sat at her bedside, and Daddy paced the floor as we cried together. I had never before seen tears on my dad's face, nor my mother swayed by anything. The grief in our home was unbearable.

The next morning neighbors came bearing food, but no one felt like eating. At every other time in our lives, Mama had been there to wipe away our tears and reassure us, but today we only had one another. Mama was inconsolable; she was no longer there. Even the preacher's words fell on deaf ears. Life would never again be the same.

Ed had made Mama laugh, and now the laughter was gone from our house. Truthfully, I'm not sure Mama would have recovered, but that God was true to His Word. He promises that He won't give us more than we can bear: "All you need to remember is that God will never let you down; he'll never let you be pushed past your limit; he'll always be there to help you come through it" (1 Corinthians 10:13, *The Message*). When Mama was brought to the point of despair, God intervened—though not in a way that any of us would have predicted.

God deals with each of us as individuals. He knew that Mama loved her children with all of her heart, and He also knew that she didn't possess the strength to overcome this tragedy on her own. We girls were old enough to take care of ourselves, and Mama knew we had one another, so we weren't enough to lure her from her grief. God knew that only one thing could lift our mother from utter hopelessness—and that was another child who needed her. You guessed it—soon after Ed's death, Mama learned she was pregnant.

At first she reacted in anger. How could God possibly believe that a baby could replace her beloved son? Then fear made its entrance: "How can I take care of a baby?" we heard her ask family and friends in desperation. No one had the answers—Mama's grief was so consuming that she still couldn't get out of bed.

But then came Joy. When our baby sister was born, Daddy gave her that nickname to reflect exactly what she meant to all of us. Joy forced Mama to heal because she needed a mommy. Mama had to put aside her grief to nurture the new life she'd been given. In the years that followed, she marveled many times, "The Lord knew how to reach me—through the baby."

In time, the pain and grief dimmed. Little Joy brought smiles back into our home—she even made my mother laugh! Though we will never forget Ed or completely recover from his passing, Joy made life bright again.

When our parents died, my sisters and I felt grief *and* relief—we knew that they had been reunited with Ed. God has wiped away every tear, and the mourning is finally over. And we know that we will join them one day.

My friend's story reflects a beautiful truth: Life overcomes death. It always has, and it always will.

> *Although the world is full of suffering,*
> *it is full also of the overcoming of it.*
> HELEN KELLER

THE HAPPIEST HOLIDAY

My friend Jean Mitchell fought to live harder than anyone I've ever known. A victim of breast cancer while still in her thirties, she had two young children and wanted desperately to watch them grow up and to guide them through life.

But it was not to be. Although she lived two years longer than the doctor predicted, it wasn't nearly long enough for those of us who knew and loved her.

Jean and I had played in the same bridge club since our college days. One November, although only she knew it, she joined us to play her last game. It is hard to believe when I remember how she was that night—she was very positive, and full of smiles. I'm sure she had to be in excruciating pain, but she never let us know.

We were given only a hint when she told us quietly, "I won't be able to have the Christmas party at my house this year." Our bridge club celebrated Christmas by exchanging homemade gifts and holding a cookie swap. Jean enjoyed Christmas more than anyone I've ever known. She created beautiful gifts and always hosted our annual party. She would decorate her entire house for the party, constructing a true winter wonderland inside. We all marveled at her creativity and her talent.

Though Jean appeared to be feeling all right, we weren't surprised that she didn't feel up to hosting the party. Another club member volunteered her home, and the matter was settled.

A couple of days before our party, Jean's husband called to say he was taking Jean to the hospital. Charlie told me that the cancer had spread to Jean's brain and that she could no longer function at home. We were all devastated, especially when we realized that she was going to miss the Christmas party she had always loved so much.

Charlie told us that, true to her love of Christmas, before she left for the hospital she wrapped all of the gifts she had made for us. He wanted to drop them by. We hurriedly wrapped up our gifts for her and sent them on with him to the hospital.

On that particular year, Meg was spending Christmas Eve with her dad. Since I would be alone, I volunteered to be with Jean at the hospital that night so that Charlie could spend an evening with his children. I had an early dinner with friends, then called the hospital to tell Charlie I was on my way.

"I'm sorry," the receptionist said gently. "Your friend died a short while ago."

I ached inside, knowing that Jean wanted to see Christmas Day, her favorite of the year. It seemed so sad to think that at her house from now on, Christmas Eve would be marred by the memory of her death.

I carried my disappointment to the Lord. *I just don't understand this,* I told Him. *Couldn't You have waited until after Christmas to take Jean home?* The thought of her husband and two young children grieving haunted me as I prayed for them.

When I returned home that night, I pulled out my Bible, searching for answers to alleviate my grief. I read the passages on peace and eternal life and was comforted to think that my friend was no longer in pain and had gone to heaven.

I still anguished over the timing of her death and realized that I might never understand. "Now we see things imperfectly as in a poor mirror, but then we will see everything with perfect clarity. All that I know now is partial and incomplete, but then I will know everything completely, just as God knows me now" (1 Corinthians 13:12, NLT). As I went to bed that night, this verse's truth soothed my frustration. I didn't understand God's decision, but I knew in my heart that He never overlooked any detail. I could trust Him in that.

When Meg returned home from her dad's house the next morning, I had Christmas all ready for her. Our tradition was to begin by reading the Christmas story. As I turned to Luke, a verse stood out: "Suddenly a great company of the heavenly host appeared with the angel, praising God and saying, 'Glory to God in the highest, and on earth peace to men on whom his favor rests'" (Luke 2:13–14). I realized suddenly that heaven was the greatest of all places to be on Christmas Day, to celebrate the birthday of our Savior. God had given Jean a great gift by taking her home for her favorite day of the year. At this very moment she was enjoying Christmas with One who had been born in human flesh in a manger so that she could one day live with Him forever—how very fitting, and how lovely!

Our God is kind, and He holds us safely in His will. Jesus told us, "My sheep listen to my voice; I know them, and they follow me. I give them eternal life, and they shall never perish; no one can snatch them out of my hand. My Father, who has given them to me, is greater than all; no one can snatch them out of my Father's hand" (John 10:27–29).

Sorrow fully accepted brings its own gifts.
For there is an alchemy in sorrow.
It can be transmuted into wisdom, which,
if it does not bring joy, can yet bring happiness.

PEARL S. BUCK

PROMISES TO STAND ON

Promise: Mourners will be comforted. "You're blessed when you feel you've lost what is most dear to you. Only then you can be embraced by the One most dear to you" (Matthew 5:4, *The Message*).

Do the words of this verse startle you? Do you feel anything *but* blessed today? Does grief over the loss of a loved one leave you overwhelmed by sorrow, disinterested even in going through the motions? If so, this verse is exactly tailored to you. It specifically addresses those who are swallowed up by pain, and it offers the promise of true comfort. How can you feel God's embrace in these dark days?

First, stay in the Word to understand God and His compassion. Read stories pertaining to God's faithfulness, such as Judges 6 (Gideon and his battles) and 1 Kings 17 (Elijah and the ravens).

Second, pray—even when you feel your words are doing nothing but exiting your mouth. Realize that the stamina you need lies not within you, but within Him: "Look to the LORD and *his* strength; seek his face always" (Psalm 105:4, emphasis mine). If you can't find the words, God will provide them. Peruse the Psalms and pray them.

> LORD, have mercy on me.
> See how I suffer....
> Snatch me back from the jaws of death.
> PSALM 9:13, NLT

> Bend down, O LORD, and hear my prayer;
> answer me, for I need your help.
> Protect me, for I am devoted to you.
> Save me, for I serve you and trust you.
> You are my God.
> PSALM 86:1–2, NLT

I am losing all hope;
  I am paralyzed with fear.
I remember the days of old.
  I ponder all your great works.
I think about what you have done.
  I reach out for you.
I thirst for you as parched land thirsts for rain.

PSALM 143:4–6, NLT

The psalmist reminds us that Israel "cried to the LORD in their trouble, and he saved them from their distress. He sent forth his word and healed them; he rescued them from the grave" (Psalm 107:19–20). We, God's newly chosen people, can count on His strength in the same way. Friend, watch for His help; wait for it; expect it. It will come.

Confidence…is directness and courage in meeting the facts of life.

JOHN DEWEY

Promise: God's love is still at work.

Do you think anyone is going to be able to drive a wedge between us and Christ's love for us? There is no way! Not trouble, not hard times, not hatred, not hunger, not homelessness, not bullying threats, not backstabbing, not even the worst sins listed in Scripture…. None of this fazes us because Jesus loves us. I'm absolutely convinced that nothing—nothing living or dead, angelic or demonic, today or tomorrow, high or low, thinkable or unthinkable—absolutely *nothing* can get between us and God's love because of the way that Jesus our Master has embraced us. (Romans 8:35, 37–39, *The Message*)

The fact is that even the deepest pain cannot separate you from God's love. You may not feel it or see it; it may seem as distant as the loved one you grieve today. But your senses are not accurate reporters: God's love is real and alive and at work, whether the evidence is tangible or not. The best way to know this—to find the warmth of His embrace in the chill of grief—is to surround yourself with people who love you. In their arms, know Jesus' closeness. In their kindness, recognize God's sympathy for your pain. In their helpfulness, see God acting on your behalf. When loving friends offer their presence, accept it.

Join a support group. Fellow grievers can best understand your feelings, your highs and lows, your hopelessness. They can also relate how they are surviving and give you helpful ideas. Finding others in the same situation may help you feel less alone, and these new friends are gifts from God for your journey through grief. The comfort they bring comes from Him.

Help others. Think of someone who could use an encouraging note, a fresh bouquet of flowers, a warm batch of cookies. In the early days of grief, you may not be able to accomplish this—you may need all of your strength just to cope with the shock of your loss. This is normal and okay. But as weeks and months pass, take a little time to consider who else might need your comfort, however limited it may be.

Even if you focus on something besides the pain for only a few minutes, it is a healthy step. The high school in our town, Pacific Palisades, has a program in which the elderly tutor struggling students. The efforts of these tutors have changed and inspired lives. The Bible suggests that such activities reverberate in surprising ways: "A generous man will prosper; he who refreshes others will himself be refreshed" (Proverbs 11:25).

As you utilize the love of friends and fellow mourners and reach out to others who are burdened, you will discover that God's love is still lighting your pathway. The darkness of grief is murky but not impenetrable, and God's presence is always near.

> *Courage is the power to let go of the familiar.*
> RAYMOND LINDQUIST

Promise: God Himself will bring you healing. "The God of all grace, who called you to his eternal glory in Christ, after you have suffered a little while, will himself restore you and make you strong, firm and steadfast. To him be the power for ever and ever" (1 Peter 5:10–11).

You've probably heard the phrase "Three steps forward, two steps back." This applies to grief. Just when you think you're finally moving forward, you find yourself again swamped by pain, back in the place you started. But have you ever considered the true meaning of the words? Even if you take three steps forward and then two back, you are still progressing. You will eventually arrive at your intended destination, slowly but surely. In the process of grieving, try to deal with only one day at a time. Hang on, and remember— you're still moving.

Here are some grief busters to help get you through the difficult days ahead.

- Praise the Lord. This may seem like a mean assignment. When you are grieving, what could seem more impossible than thanking God for anything? But it's important. Even if you don't feel praise in your heart, praise with your lips. A widowed friend of mine determined to praise God for one thing every single day. That is a wonderful start. It keeps the eyes of your heart peeled for God's goodness.
- Seek joy. Anything that brings you a twinge of pleasure is worth the time spent seeking it out. It may be viewing a glorious sunset, gazing at a photograph and recalling happy

days, listening to the lilting voice of your grandchild, or strolling through a beautiful garden.

- Smile. Find someone to smile at today, even if it's only the mail carrier. If you do not go out at all, smile at yourself in the mirror. Think of something that brings a smile to your lips and your heart. You want to stay in practice, because smiling will one day again be a natural reaction!

- Create a special time just for you each day. Pamper yourself: Soak in a hot bath; treat yourself to a manicure; enjoy the luxury of an afternoon nap.

- Do unto others. Do something special for someone else, something that you would enjoy being done for you. Write a letter, share a reminiscence, bake an enticing treat, or invite someone over for a hot cup of tea. This exercise will take your mind off your pain, even if for just a short while.

- Spread your wings and try a new adventure. When you again have the energy, enroll in the art class you've always wanted to take or make a scrapbook containing special photos and memories for your children. Take up gardening—begin with a single potted plant and watch it flourish.

- Take a prayer walk. Go alone, or invite a friend along. As you walk, pray for your needs and thank God for His blessings. If you don't feel up to walking around the neighborhood, then take a few steps around your house. The exercise will help to clear your mind, refresh your spirit, and energize your body.

The greatest test of courage on earth
is to bear defeat without losing heart.
ROBERT G. INGERSOLL

CONCLUSION:
THE HOUSE ON THE ROCK STANDS FIRM

Does it seem as though you're trudging through storm clouds, buffeted by assaulting winds, shaken from your foundation? If your life is God's, you may feel removed from all that is friendly and familiar, but you are still safe. This storm will not conquer you. God's light will return.

Remember Jesus' parable: "Everyone who hears these words of mine and puts them into practice is like a wise man who built his house on the rock. The rain came down, the streams rose, and the winds blew and beat against that house; yet it did not fall, because it had its foundation on the rock" (Matthew 7:24–25). This man's story had a happy ending, and yours can, too.

God does not forsake us in our grief; in fact, He sometimes intervenes in unusual ways to comfort us.

Consider the story of actor and actress Ed Binns and Elizabeth Franz. Ed, who had recently survived a bout with cancer, invited his wife, Elizabeth, to drive with him to a nearby town for afternoon tea.

Pausing at a stop sign, Ed inhaled deeply. "Elizabeth," he said, "have you ever seen such a beautiful sunset in all your life?"

Elizabeth looked at Ed questioningly; it was raining outside. Joy lit his face as he laid his head back and sighed. It was the last breath he took. In Ed's final moments on earth, God had provided comfort for Elizabeth.

My friend Lucille experienced the storm of grief when her husband, George, died of complications following a car accident. Self-pity threatened to overtake Lucille. She found herself asking the Lord, *Why didn't You take me first?* She knew that God had given her the instruction in His Word, "The widow who is really in need and left all alone puts her hope in God and continues night and day to pray and to ask God for help" (1 Timothy 5:5). So she prayed through her anguish.

Lucille broke her leg a few days before her ninetieth birthday. She felt more depressed than ever. *If only George were here,* she thought helplessly. *He could have washed away my blues with his wise and encouraging words.*

On one particularly dark day, Lucille telephoned a friend and asked her to come visit. When her friend said she was unable to come, Lucille began to weep. She prayed, *Dear God, please give me the strength to get through this hour.*

A quiet voice responded with, *Get your Bible.* Lucille's Bible was in her bedroom, too far away for her to retrieve with the bulky cast on her leg. Then she remembered seeing a travel Bible in the living room. She opened it up—and was shocked when she discovered that it was George's; she thought she had given his away.

Lucille turned to her favorite passage. Suddenly, a letter sifted into her lap—it was a love letter from George. His words of comfort soothed Lucille's aching heart.

As her tears flowed, Lucille continued leafing through the Bible. Sure enough—more notes from George. According to the dates, he had written them prior to an earlier surgery. Apparently he had feared that he would not return home; once he did, the notes and letter had been forgotten.

Then Lucille realized: *No, they were never forgotten.* God knew exactly where George's thoughts were stored, and He gifted Lucille when she needed them the most. She spent the remainder of the day alternately laughing and crying, refreshed by the company of her husband and her Lord. She had never felt less alone. "The LORD watches over the alien and sustains the fatherless and the widow" (Psalm 146:9).

Friend, continue to reach for God's hand. Let the hurricane of grief wash away everything except for the faith that He will see you through. As you stand on the Rock, you *will* outlast the storm.

Tears are a river that take you somewhere....
Tears lift your boat off the rocks, off dry ground,
carrying it downriver to someplace new, someplace better.
CLARISSA PINKOLA ESTÉS

WE WIN!

Be of good cheer; I have overcome the world.

JOHN 16:33, KJV

As a child I thought of God as sitting on a big throne, constantly watching over me and ready at any moment to jump to my defense. I imagined that He was up there in heaven at my disposal, a 9-1-1 God. Never mind that when I became overly busy, I didn't take the time to pray or read my Bible; I called on God only when I found myself up to my elbows in alligators. He was my God of convenience.

There weren't many times in my young life that I needed Him. Perhaps when I had a tough exam to take, or wanted to win an election, or when some bratty boy in my class was bullying me, or when I longed for a shiny new bike for Christmas—then I would pray. If anyone was mean to me, I wanted my heavenly Father to come down off His throne and punch him in the nose on my behalf. If I really desired something, I wanted God to wave His wand and make it suddenly appear. This was my childlike vision of God—always ready to bless the good guys and zap the bad ones.

Now that I've lived for half a century, I confess that I had a hard time letting go of the myth of God as fairy godfather. I still want Him to annihilate the evil people and protect the good ones. I still want

Him to overpower every obstacle in my life and bless me richly with everything I desire. But fifty years have shown me that neither life nor God works that way. While He promised His presence, He chooses whether or not to intercept tragedy. As we've seen in these chapters, terrible things do happen, and God allows it. But He never leaves us alone to deal with the outcome.

It was always of great comfort to me when my minister in Atlanta, Dr. Paul Walker, said, "I've read the last chapter in the Book, and I know that in the end we win!" This is really all we need to know. In whatever trial you are walking through at the moment, in whatever disappointments you are facing, in whatever storms are trying to blow you from your faith, you will be victorious if you are committed to your Lord and Savior.

Consider how Goliath daunted the Israelites. They were terrified of him! But how did David approach the giant? With confidence. With certainty. With clout—after all, he had God on his side! When Saul questioned the young man's abilities, David responded, "The LORD who delivered me from the paw of the lion and the paw of the bear will deliver me from the hand of this Philistine" (1 Samuel 17:37).

How did David acquire this tremendous faith in the heavenly Father? Pure and simple: David had spent his years as a shepherd getting to know God intimately. He had experienced the Lord's power and exercised his faith until it was a strong muscle. He had spent time alone with his Creator and knew what he could expect of Him. Even though a situation might appear hopeless, frightening, even life threatening, David knew what God he served. Do you?

I hope this book helps you come to know Him better. God allows storms in our lives to prepare us for His work in this world. When God wants to use people, He will allow them to land in the midst of a struggle to build their strength and their witness.

Do you recall how peaceful the earth feels after a storm? The

moisture on the leaves glistens like crystals in the sunli
shine breaks through, chasing away the dark clouds. The
Quiet descends, broken only by the sounds of singing
out from beneath their shelter.

So it is in our lives. After we have survived the stor
ence an incredible peace from the Lord that allows
firmly the next time a storm brews in our
new meaning, and the things that
are more ready to help others who a
better empathize with the grieving than a
loss? Who can offer encouragement through a
who has already suffered and seen victory throug.

A storm survivor is like a beacon, shining brilliantly through
howling winds and pelting rain. She stands as an example to Christian
brothers and sisters, offering hope and encouragement. She who has
experienced the Lord's strength can better share the light she received
by standing on God's promises.

As a survivor, let me tell you today that no matter who is taking
advantage of you or what is going wrong in your life, know that in the
end all the bad guys will be destroyed, every wrong will be righted,
every tear will be dried, and good will win out over evil. Your Goliath
will fall. You can believe this because you know that God is so much
more than a fairy godfather. He is a loving King, a tender Shepherd, a
kind and powerful Presence in a harsh world.

Friend, while the storm rages, take shelter in His embrace; accept
His comfort; know His direction; discover His faithfulness. He is a
heavenly Father who loves His children. Just as my favorite hymn by
Gloria and Bill Gaither proclaims, "Because He lives, I can face tomorrow!" You, too, can face tomorrow because our Savior lives forever
and ever. The prophet Isaiah wisely wrote, "You have been a refuge for
the poor, a refuge for the needy in his distress, a shelter from the storm
and a shade from the heat" (Isaiah 25:4).

Notes

C H A P T E R 2
B. Smedes, *The Art of Forgiving: When You Need to Don't Know How* (Nashville, Tenn.: Moorings, 1996), xii,

C H A P T E R 3
1. Elisabeth Elliot, *Loneliness* (Nashville, Tenn.: Oliver-Nelson Books, 1988), 140. This book has been retitled *The Path of Loneliness*.

C H A P T E R 6
1. Norman Vincent Peale, *Three Complete Books: A Guide to Confident Living, Stay Alive All Your Life, The Amazing Effects of Positive Thinking* (New York: Random House, 1996), 143–4.

C H A P T E R 7
1.0 Mrs. Charles E. Cowman, *Streams in the Desert 1* (Grand Rapids: Zondervan, 1965), 16–7.

C H A P T E R 8
1. Elisabeth Elliot, *Loneliness* (Nashville, Tenn.: Oliver-Nelson Books, 1988), 18.

Multnomah Publishers ®
The publisher and author would love to hear your comments about this book. *Please contact us at:*
www.multnomah.net/standingonthepromises